12.00

YOUTH**WALK** again™

Other Books in This Series

Youthwalk:
Sex, Parents, Popularity,
and Other Topics for Teen Survival

More Youthwalk:
Faith, Dating, Friendship,
and Other Topics for Teen Survival

Your Daily Walk:
365 Daily Devotions to Read
Through the Bible in a Year

Closer Walk:
365 Daily Devotions that Nurture
a Heart for God

Family Walk:
Love, Anger, Courage, and 49 Other
Weekly Readings for Your Family Devotions

More Family Walk:
Habits, Fairness, Stress, and 49 Other
Weekly Readings for Your Family Devotions

Family Walk Again:
Family, Friends, Self-esteem, and 49 Other
Weekly Readings for Your Family Devotions

YOUTHWALK again™

Bruce H. Wilkinson
Executive Editor

Len Woods
Editor

Paula A. Kirk
General Editor

Walk Thru the Bible Ministries
Atlanta, Georgia

Zondervan Publishing House
Grand Rapids, Michigan

Youthwalk Again
Self-esteem, Stress, Forgiveness, and Other Topics for Teens
Copyright © 1993 by Walk Thru the Bible Ministries
All rights reserved

Published by Zondervan Publishing House

Requests for information should be addressed to:
Walk Thru the Bible Ministries   or   Zondervan Publishing House
4201 North Peachtree Road   Grand Rapids, MI 49530
Atlanta, GA 30341–1207

Library of Congress Cataloging-in-Publication Data

Youthwalk Again: self-esteem, stress, forgiveness, and other topics for
teen survival/ Walk Thru the Bible Ministries, Atlanta, Georgia
    p. cm.
    Summary: Another collection of daily devotional readings to help
young people deal with common problems and concerns
    ISBN 0-310-54601-X
    1. Teenagers—Prayer-books and devotions—English. 2. Self-respect—
Religious aspects—Christianity. I. Walk Thru the Bible (Educational
Ministry) II. Title: Youthwalk Again.
BV4850.Y683   1993   93—17217
242'.63—dc20   CIP

Cover and interior design by Michelle Beeman
Cover photo by Kevin Johnson
Illustrations by J. Michael Leonard and Dan Nelson
Photography by Kevin Johnson and Norhill Photography

Printed in the United States of America

93 94 95 96 / RRD / 10 9 8 7 6 5 4 3 2 1

Dedication

In every generation leaders arise who seem larger than life. While they are pilgrims like the rest of us, and would be the last to see themselves as different, they nonetheless are. God has commissioned Dr. James Dobson, and his faithful wife Shirley, to lead the charge in our day to protect the American family, and especially its vulnerable teenagers. As parents who have raised faithful young people themselves and are helping millions of parents do the same, we dedicate *Youthwalk Again* to Jim and Shirley Dobson.

Bruce H. Wilkinson

Acknowledgments

Youthwalk Again: Stress, Self-esteem, Forgiveness, and Other Topics for Teen Survival is the third compilation of topical studies from *Youthwalk,* a magazine for teens published monthly by Walk Thru the Bible Ministries. We thank the many folks who have helped us over the years, especially all the teens, youth leaders, and parents who made up our focus groups, posed for photos, and wrote articles and letters that kept us on track.

And we're especially grateful to all the people in Walk Thru the Bible's Specialized Publishing Group, from the leadership team to the staff in production.

Special thanks go to Michelle Beeman, Helen Ryser, Robyn Holmes, and Kevin Johnson, our *Youthwalk* design and production team. Also, the creative contributions of Kyle Henderson and Cary McNeal are much appreciated. All have invested their time and talents to produce a book that will make a lasting difference in the lives of young people.

Introduction

As a Christian teenager, are you sometimes confused by the modern world? Do you ever feel pressure to do things you know you shouldn't? Have you ever been asked a tough question about Christianity—and not known the answer? Are you ever embarrassed about sharing your faith?

If you answered any of those questions with a yes, I've got good news for you: You're not alone. But the book you have in your hand can help!

Youthwalk Again is carefully designed to help you understand the Bible and apply its truth to your life. *Youthwalk Again* will help you establish the Bible as your rock—your sure foundation in this unsure world. No longer will you see the Bible as a book of boring stories about things that happened eons ago. Instead, you'll see the Bible as *relevant*—a vital resource for you to live a happy, successful, and productive life.

We at Walk Thru the Bible Ministries are thrilled to join with Zondervan Publishing House to make this Bible-reading guide available to you.

Bruce H. Wilkinson
President and Executive Editor
Walk Thru the Bible Ministries

How to Get the Most Out of *Youthwalk Again*

Youthwalk Again is arranged by topics—one for each week. You can start with the first topic or just jump in at any point in the book. Just put a check in the accompanying box to keep your place.

Each topic has an introductory page (to preview the topic) and five devotional pages (one for each weekday—Monday through Friday). Each of the daily devotional pages includes the following five sections:

1. *The Opening Story*—sets up the problem

2. *Look It Up*—shows what the Bible says about the problem

3. *Think It Through*—stimulates your thinking about the problem

4. *Work It Out*—gives practical suggestions for solving the problem

5. *Nail It Down*—shares other passages where you can find more wise counsel about the problem

But that's not all! In addition to the weekly devotional topics, *Youthwalk Again* will educate, stimulate, and motivate you with these exciting features:

- *Hot Topic*—Each "Hot Topic" gives biblical answers to an important current issue.

- *Search for Satisfaction*—These pages are stories of humankind's ultimate search: a relationship with God through Jesus Christ.

- *Wide World of the Word*—These fun-filled pages are full of little-known facts about God's Word. Who said learning can't be enjoyable?

- *What on Earth Is God Like?*—These pages present the attributes of God in a down-to-earth way.

Do you want to do great things for God? Of course you do, or you wouldn't be reading this book. Follow the above instructions, and six months from now, you'll know God's Word better than you do today.

And that will be a great thing!

Walk Thru the Bible Ministries

Walk Thru the Bible Ministries (WTB) unofficially began in the early 1970s in Portland, Oregon, with the teaching of Old and New Testament surveys of the Bible. Dr. Bruce H. Wilkinson was looking for a way to innovatively teach the Word of God so that it would change people's lives.

Dr. Wilkinson officially founded WTB in 1976 as a nonprofit ministry. In 1978 WTB moved to its current home in Atlanta.

From these small beginnings WTB has grown into one of the leading Christian organizations in America with an international ministry extending to 21 countries in 30 languages. International branch offices are located in Australia, Brazil, Great Britain, Singapore, and New Zealand.

By focusing on the central themes of Scripture and their practical application to life, WTB has been able to develop and maintain wide acceptance in denominations and fellowships around the world. In addition, it has carefully initiated strategic ministry alliances with over one hundred Christian organizations and missions of wide diversity and background.

WTB has four major outreach ministries: seminars, publishing, leadership training, and video training.

The call of the Lord has been clear and consistent on Walk Thru the Bible as it strives to help fulfill the Lord's Great Commission. The highest ethics and standards of integrity are carefully practiced as Walk Thru the Bible lives out its commitment to excellence not only in ministry but also in its internal operational policies and procedures. No matter what the ministry, no matter where the ministry, WTB focuses on the Word of God and encourages people of all nations to grow in their knowledge of Him and in their unreserved obedience and service to Him.

CONTENTS

Topics

HOT TOPIC

WIDE WORLD OF THE WORD

THE SEARCH FOR SATISFACTION

VIEWPOINT

★ ★ ★ ★ SELF-ESTEEM ★ ★ ★ ★ ★
The War Between the "States"

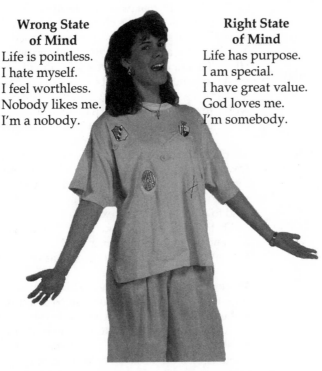

Wrong State of Mind
Life is pointless.
I hate myself.
I feel worthless.
Nobody likes me.
I'm a nobody.

Right State of Mind
Life has purpose.
I am special.
I have great value.
God loves me.
I'm somebody.

Life won't really take off for you until you get the "right" perspective about yourself. Would you like to find out more?

"Think of yourself with sober judgment" (Romans 12:3).

★ ★

E mergency room personnel worked feverishly to save the thin patient—a 17-year-old high school junior named Davey. About 45 minutes earlier, Davey had taken a .38 pistol, put it to his head, and pulled the trigger.

Police found this note at the scene: "I can't stand it anymore. We're all alone in a cold, dark universe. Life makes no sense. Since no one can give me a reason to live, I'm checking out. Please play *The Wall* at my funeral. Davey."

The deadliness of despair

Look It Up: Davey's cry of despair is joined by thousands of other young voices all over the world: "Life is pointless!" As Christians our response has to be: "No! Life has purpose!" And we need to be fully prepared to explain why we believe that.

• The Bible tells of a Deity who created us. "Then God said, 'Let us make man in our image, in our likeness'" (Genesis 1:26). We didn't evolve by random selection. We were specially designed and created by God.

• The Bible also explains that God personally involves Himself in our lives when we allow Him to. What is even more incredible is that God has a special purpose for our lives: "And we know that in all things God works for the good of those who love him, who have been called according to his purpose" (Romans 8:28).

Think It Through: If you take God out of the equation, Davey is right—nothing matters. There are no absolutes to anchor us. We spin pointlessly in eternal space with no reason to hope for anything beyond death. And to what do owe our existence? Blind chance.

On the other hand, if you recognize God's true nature and anchor your life to Him, everything makes sense. We have purpose, and our existence has real meaning.

Work It Out: You don't have to live with negative feelings about yourself. Take some steps to improve your self-esteem in a big way. Begin today by praying:

"God, I'm so glad that You are real—that we're not all alone in the cosmos. Help me to base my feelings about myself on the fact that You created me in Your image. Thank You for being at work in my life. Help me to see Your purpose for my life. Amen."

Nail It Down: Read Psalm 57:2.

★ ★ ★ ★ ★ ★ ★ ONE **SELF-ESTEEM** ★

Liz Richmond was supposed to pick up her friend, Robyn, 15 minutes ago. Crying, she buries her face in a pillow. Her mother enters the room.

"Honey, you look fine—really you do."

"No I don't, Mother! My hair looks stupid and my face is all broken out! Besides, look at my eyes now—they're all red and swollen!"

"I bet if you washed your face and—"

"Mother, it'll just be the same old story. I'll walk in with Robyn and everyone will rave about how cute she is. And I'll just be ignored!"

What the mirror doesn't show you

Look It Up: One of the hardest things to believe is the Bible's declaration that each one of us is specially designed by God:

"For you created my inmost being; you knit me together in my mother's womb. I praise you because I am fearfully and wonderfully made; your works are wonderful, I know that full well" (Psalm 139:13-14).

According to this amazing passage, you are a one-of-a-kind, original masterpiece. You have been beautifully designed (i.e. "knit together") by God.

Think It Through: Do you really believe that? Or are you constantly comparing yourself with others—top fashion models or all the studs of the silver screen—and feeling like a loser?

Comparisons are both stifling and stupid. The Rocky Mountains aren't better than the Smoky Mountains. Each mountain range is beautiful—in its own unique way.

Work It Out: Some practical tips for overcoming the "I'm so ugly" syndrome:

• Seek to look your best. Ask a parent or a Christian friend to help you think of ways—within reason—to enhance your looks.

• Take the best advice, go for it, then relax—knowing you've done all you can do.

• Most important, work on improving your spiritual appearance (1 Samuel 16:7). Remember that God values inner beauty. Many people who are merely average in physical appearance are incredibly attractive to others. Why? Because these individuals have radiant walks with Christ. They're full of His life, and nothing is more beautiful than that!

Nail It Down: Read Ephesians 2:10.

Pray About It:

★ ★ ★ ★ ★ **TWO**

3

Mark's oldest brother, right out of college, makes $40,000 a year as a computer programmer.

Mark's older sister just received an academic scholarship to Yale.

Mark's junior brother was just named to the All-State baseball team.

And Mark? Well, he flips hamburgers for $3.35 an hour, gets straight Cs, and has never made any kind of sports team. His interest is poetry. Thinking that weird, his parents constantly nag: "Do something worthwhile. Be like one of your brothers."

Is it any wonder that Mark feels worthless?

God's MVPs (much valued people)

Look It Up: Listen up—no matter what parents, coaches, teachers, or others say—you are extremely valuable to God. He cares deeply about you. Are you ready for the evidence?

• You are constantly in God's thoughts (Psalm 139:17-18).

• God keeps track of all your hurts (Psalm 56:8).

• Because you are so precious to Him, God is aware of every detail of your life: "Are not five sparrows sold for two pennies? Yet not one of them is forgotten by God. Indeed, the very hairs of your head are all numbered. Don't be afraid; you are worth more than many sparrows" (Luke 12:6-7).

What do you say to all that?

Think It Through: Society says you have worth if you are beautiful or smart or talented or can contribute to society in some way. This explains why illiterate, handicapped, poor, and elderly people are considered to be of little value. God says you matter just because you are created in His image. That's all. You don't have to do anything. You just have to be.

Work It Out: First, praise God that your worth is not dependent on what you do. He values you just because you're you.

Second, thank God for caring about every aspect of your life. (A big boost to your self-esteem comes when you realize that God is deeply concerned about you and how you feel.)

Third, go out of your way to let others know how valuable they are. Tell someone today how much God cares for him or her.

Nail It Down: Read Matthew 16:26 for more insight about your value to God.

★ ★ ★ ★ ★ **THREE** **SELF-ESTEEM** ★

Marcy fidgets nervously as the counselor begins: "Marcy, your parents are really worried about you. They say you won't talk to them. I've heard their side of the story. Now I want to hear what you're thinking. What's going on inside? Tell me how you feel."

At first, Marcy makes small talk. But soon she breaks down; her eyes overflow with tears as she sobs uncontrollably. "I just want them to love me! Is that asking too much? I don't want all the stuff—the cars and clothes. I just want to feel like they accept me the way I am!"

The greatest love of all

Look It Up: Our deepest desire? To feel completely loved. Yet with imperfect parents, sweethearts, and friends, we often feel more rejected than accepted. And that's devastating to our self-esteem. But look:

"How great is the love the Father has lavished on us, that we should be called children of God! And that is what we are!" (1 John 3:1).

In God we find the total acceptance we're craving. He doesn't just like us a little. He doesn't just love us when we act right. He "lavishes" His love on us. He pours it out abundantly.

Think It Through: Do you have parents like Marcy's who give you everything but love? Because of a divorce, the break-up of a romance, or because you're new in town, do you think: "Nobody loves me. People don't accept me. I'm worthless"?

What does 1 John 3:1 say? In what ways has God poured out His love on you?

Work It Out: If you do these things, your self-image will undoubtedly improve:

• Quit focusing on feelings. Feelings are real and important, but they don't always reflect the truth. For example, you may feel unloved, but God loves you unconditionally.

• Focus on the facts of God's Word. Get together with a friend and look up all the verses you can find that mention how much God loves and accepts His children.

• Help a friend or classmate who is feeling the same way you are. Use what you have learned from God's Word to encourage that person. It's amazing how building up someone else can refresh your own spirit.

Nail It Down: Read Ephesians 2:4-5.

Pray About It:

★ ★ ★ ★ ★ FOUR

5

Ray isn't particularly liked at school, but he isn't disliked, either. People just ignore him. Once he tried helping out with a class project. He left when the "cool" people there seemed to act as if he were invisible. Now he just hangs out with a couple of other kids who are in the same situation.

Says Ray, "You want to know how I feel? I'll bet if I left school today and never came back, nobody—not even the teachers—would notice."

Friends in high places

Look It Up: Feeling like a nobody hurts. We want to feel like people know us and that we matter to them. But God knows all about us and we matter to Him apart from what anyone else thinks:

• "But the man who loves God is known by God" (1 Corinthians 8:3).

• Jesus said, " 'I am the good shepherd; I know my sheep and my sheep know me' " (John 10:14).

The truth is that when we trust Christ, all heaven rejoices (Luke 15:7), and our names are inscribed in heaven's "book of life" (Luke 10:20).

Do you see what that means? You may feel like a stranger in some places, but the fact is, in heaven you already belong.

Think It Through: Why be down on yourself when the God of the universe isn't down on you? He says you are loved and accepted and that your life has a purpose. Christians with poor self-images are actually saying, "Sorry, God, but You're wrong. You're either lying or mistaken when You say all those things about me."

Work It Out: Pick out one verse this week that has meant the most to you and memorize it. Every time your self-esteem takes a dive, say it out loud.

Then find some people on the fringe—students like Ray. Help them develop better self-images by including them in your group's activities. Ministering to others not only helps them, it also provides you with a sense of purpose.

Nail It Down: Continue to improve your self-esteem by seeing how precious you are to God. On Saturday read Romans 8:31-39. On Sunday read Ephesians 1:3-14.

★ ★ ★ ★ ★ ★ FIVE **SELF-ESTEEM** ★

COMMUNICATION
Inspecting the Way You Interact

Should you read the next few pages? Only if one or more of the following is true:

(a) Your talks with family members are more like shouting matches.

(b) You feel like nobody listens to a word you say (or people say you don't listen to them).

(c) "Haphazard and harsh" describes your communication skills more accurately than "truthful and tender."

(d) You care more about friendships than about relationships at home.

If any of those descriptions fit, perhaps you'd better keep reading.

"Don't let anyone look down on you because you are young, but set an example for the believers in speech, in life, in love, in faith and in purity" (1 Timothy 4:12).

It took exactly one minute for the Rupperts' peaceful dinner to turn into World War III. It started when Mr. Ruppert innocently asked Patricia, 15, "So, what have you got planned for the weekend?" (Let's join the action in progress.)

"I told you, I don't know, Dad. Why don't you just quit picking on me? You're always nosing around in my business!"

"Hold on. Don't you raise your voice to me like that, young lady!"

"I have to. You never listen!"

"That's it! Go to your room . . . and whatever plans you had, cancel them!"

When discussions destroy

Look It Up: When did chaotic communication begin? Way back in the Garden of Eden, that's when. Adam and Eve plunged the world into sin. And now . . .

• Sin turns our focus inward. Instead of considering others, we are obsessed with ourselves. In our selfishness, we hide from others (Genesis 3:7).

• Sin fills us with uncomfortable feelings—fear, shame, and guilt. "He [Adam] answered, 'I heard you in the garden, and I was afraid because I was naked; so I hid'" (Genesis 3:10).

• Sin causes us to lash out at others and blame them for our own mistakes (Genesis 3:12-13).

Now do you see why there are so many barriers to good communication?

Think It Through: Imagine the interaction between Adam and Eve when they first got kicked out of the Garden of Eden (Genesis 3:23-24).

Did they give each other the silent treatment? Did they yell and scream? The Bible doesn't say. All we can assume is that between the end of chapter three and the beginning of chapter four, the first couple must have made up (see Genesis 4:1).

See, there is hope—even in a sinful world.

Work It Out: Do you want to learn to be a good communicator despite all of sin's obstacles? You can this week. And God will help if you ask Him:

"Lord, I understand better now why I sometimes have problems talking with my parents, brothers and sisters, and friends. Teach me the skills I need to build stronger relationships. Help me clean up my act in interacting with others. Amen."

Nail It Down: Read Proverbs 12:18.

☞ ☞ ☞ ☞ ☞ **ONE COMMUNICATION**

At school the next day, Patricia's friend, Matt, finally says, "Hey, why are you such a crab? You've been snapping at everybody all day."

"Oh," Patricia gulps. "It's my Dad. He's always on my back. Last night he asked me what my plans were for the weekend. Before I could explain to him about the party, he started firing questions at me like, 'Will they be drinking? Will there be any adults there?' And on and on. He never listens to me!"

Patricia stops and looks at Matt. He's watching some girl and not even paying attention to what she's saying!

The forgotten art of listening

Look It Up: Do you ever get the feeling that nobody—not even parents and friends—knows how to listen? Maybe we all need to listen to this verse:

"My dear brothers, take note of this: Everyone should be quick to listen, slow to speak and slow to become angry" (James 1:19).

We generally reverse things, don't we? We're quick to run our mouths and speak our minds, and slow to listen to what others are saying.

Think It Through: It's not enough just to hear the sounds that come out of someone's mouth. We must strive to understand what people are saying and why.

How would you feel if you were pouring out your heart to a friend and he or she . . .
- interrupted with his or her own story
- looked away?
- started trying to give you advice?
- looked at the clock?
- fell asleep?

Work It Out: Follow these ABCs to become a better listener:
- **A**sk friends to open up and share their feelings. Most people are dying to talk, but they don't because they realize that few people are willing to listen.
- **Be** quiet while others verbalize their thoughts. It's tough to keep your mouth shut. Concentrate hard, focusing all your attention on the speaker and on the words being spoken.
- **C**onfirm the feelings of others. Show that you understand what they mean by repeating some of their statements back to them.

Nail It Down: Read Proverbs 18:13.

Pray About It:

T W O

9

At lunch, Patricia and Shelly accidentally make eye contact —but only for a second. Each looks away immediately.

The incident causes Patricia to think back to last fall. "I can't believe Shelly got so mad at me just for riding home with Greg— as if I were trying to flirt with him or something! We were best friends, but now we don't even talk to each other. I wish she wouldn't hate me."

But Shelly misses the friendship, too: "I'd really like to be friends with Patricia again, but I know she doesn't want anything to do with me."

What to do when the lid blows off

Look It Up: When the following attitudes invade our lives, they eventually become part of our communication habits:
- Laziness (Ecclesiastes 10:18)
- Pride (Proverbs 29:23)
- Selfishness (Philippians 2:3-4)
- Bitterness—"See to it that no one misses the grace of God and that no bitter root grows up to cause trouble and defile many" (Hebrews 12:15).

Think It Through: Patricia and Shelly's conflict is such a shame. Neither one wants it. They miss each other. But because of a stupid misunderstanding they haven't spoken for over four months. If only they had talked things out.

Are there unresolved conflicts in your life? If so, wouldn't you like to get things straight?

Work It Out: Whether it's a fight with a friend, a duel with Dad, or a showdown with your sweetheart, consider these steps for conflict resolution:
- Pray for a right attitude (Ephesians 4:23) and a restored relationship.
- Take the initiative. *"If it is possible, as far as it depends on you, live at peace with everyone" (Romans 12:18).* Make the first move to restore the relationship.
- Assume personal responsibility (James 5:16). Admit guilt where you blew it. Conflicts rarely occur all because of one person.
- Avoid high voltage words. Saying "I hate it when you . . ." or "You never . . ." or "You always . . . " puts people on the defensive (Ephesians 4:29).
- Work hard to listen carefully (James 1:19) and to make yourself understood.

Nail It Down: Read Ephesians 4:31-32.

☎ ☎ ☎ ☎ ☎ **THREE COMMUNICATION** ☎

A classmate says to Patricia, "I just love Public Enemy's latest album."

Patricia mumbles, "Yeah, it's pretty good," even though she thinks most of the songs are trash.

Later that afternoon, a boy in her class (who also happens to be in her youth group) tries to be funny, but Patricia finds him irritating. She lets him have it: "Eddie, you're such a jerk! No wonder no girls want to go out with you! Why don't you just get lost?"

The "TNT" formula for dialogue

Look It Up: What are the essential ingredients of biblical communication?

1. Truthfulness—"Each of you must put off falsehood and speak truthfully to his neighbor" (Ephesians 4:25).

2. Tenderness—"Instead, speaking the truth in love, we will in all things grow up into him who is the Head, that is, Christ" (Ephesians 4:15).

Truthfulness and tenderness—put them together and you've got "TNT" strong enough to blow away the most destructive dialogue!

Think It Through: The "TNT" formula (truthfulness + tenderness) can be found even in secular sources:

• A Billy Joel tune says: *"Honesty is such a lonely word—everyone is so untrue. Honesty is hardly ever heard, and mostly what I need from you."*

• There's more to communication than the words we say. It's also about *how* we say them—tone of voice and body language.

Work It Out: Evaluate the truth content of your communication. Do you:

• shade the truth when your parents ask questions?
• rationalize wrong actions to God?
• hide your true feelings because you're afraid?

Stop those dishonest actions and make the tough commitment to speak the truth today.

Now evaluate how tender your communication is. Are you:

• extremely critical of certain people?
• so blunt that you frequently hurt the feelings of others? Ask God to give you more sensitivity.

Nail It Down: Read Proverbs 27:5-6.

Pray About It:

FOUR

L ast night Shelly got a phone call from her youth pastor. He said, "I was just calling to let you know how much I appreciate your participation in youth group. It really means a lot to look out there and see your smiling face every week. Thanks."

Then after school she was feeling down because of a failed pop quiz in geography. Someone handed her a note. It said, "Don't feel too bad—I flunked too. Want to get a pizza? Love, Patricia."

Building wisely with constructive words

Look It Up: The New Testament lists different types of constructive communication. Christians are to:

• Instruct—teach others about God's truth (2 Timothy 3:16).

• Admonish—Admonition refers to correcting or warning those involved in wrong behavior. "We proclaim him, admonishing and teaching everyone with all wisdom, so that we may present everyone perfect in Christ" (Colossians 1:28).

• Exhort—strongly urge others to do what is right (Hebrews 10:24).

• Encourage—stimulate, spur on, or hearten those who are discouraged (1 Thessalonians 5:14).

• Comfort—cheer or console those who hurt (2 Corinthians 1:3-4).

Think It Through: Think about the communication verbs above. Which one is the hardest to do? Which one is the easiest? Do you need someone to communicate with you in one of those ways? Which one?

Work It Out: There are a number of things you can do to become involved in constructive communication.

• Share a Bible verse with a friend who's down.

• Help out at church by teaching the little kids in Sunday school or junior church.

• Call a Christian friend who's straying from the faith, and invite him or her to lunch. Express your concern, and admonish your friend to "keep in step with the Spirit" (Galatians 5:25).

Nail It Down: Read Hebrews 3:13. On Saturday read Proverbs 12:6, and on Sunday spend a few minutes memorizing that verse.

☎ ☎ ☎ ☎ ☎ FIVE **COMMUNICATION** ☎

MEDIA

66 66 66 66 66 66 66   99 99 99 99 99 99 99 99 99

Mass Communication or Mass Manipulation?

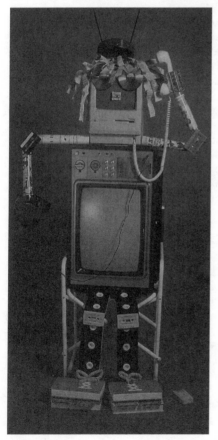

Not one of us goes a day without exposure to some form of mass communication in newspapers, magazines, books, radio, television, or movies. If we're not careful about what we read, hear, and watch, we can be subtly manipulated. That's because many non-biblical messages are being communicated.

For a look at some of the ways the media influence us, meet Derek, Amy, Chris, Kelley, and Walter—members of the Pratt Academy Media Club.

"Finally, brothers, whatever is true, whatever is noble, whatever is right, whatever is pure, whatever is lovely, whatever is admirable—if anything is excellent or praiseworthy—think about such things" (Philippians 4:8).

99 99 99 99 99 99 99 99 99 99 99 99 99 99 99 99 99 99 99 99 99 99 99 99 99 99

Let's meet our first Media Club member:

Derek Dillard, age 16. Distinction: Most horror flicks seen by any teenager east of Death Valley. Aspiration: To be the next Stephen King.

"Gory stuff doesn't bug me," Derek brags. "I've got a cast-iron stomach."

He's seen the entire *Nightmare on Elm Street* series (he's even got a "Freddy" poster on his wall) and every installment of *Friday the 13th* at least twice. His all-time favorite is *Halloween*.

Claims Derek, "Nothing beats a plate of nachos and a good horror flick on Saturday night."

Blood and guts drive you nuts!

Look It Up: Does the Bible have a word for Derek (and for us)? Most certainly.

• "Do not envy a violent man or choose any of his ways, for the LORD detests a perverse man but takes the upright into his confidence" (Proverbs 3:31-32).

• "From the fruit of his lips a man enjoys good things, but the unfaithful have a craving for violence" (Proverbs 13:2).

• "The violence of the wicked will drag them away, for they refuse to do what is right" (Proverbs 21:7).

It doesn't take an Einstein to look at these verses and realize that God disapproves of violence—and that includes the violence portrayed in the media.

Think It Through: Lately Derek has become insensitive to violence; it just doesn't bother him anymore. The other day he watched two guys beat up a classmate after school. His reaction was, "That's life!"

If you think constant exposure to "blood and guts" (even if it's all fake) doesn't affect people, how do you respond to the numerous studies that conclusively link media violence with aggressive, hostile behavior?

Work It Out: Take action against the violence in your life! Refuse to go to slasher movies (like those named above) that specialize in torture and death. Reject heavy metal and punk bands—like W.A.S.P., Venom, Iron Maiden, and Guns 'N Roses—that glamorize aggressive, brutal behavior. And encourage your friends to do the same.

Copy the verse on the previous page on an index card and carry it around with you this week. Memorize it and make it a goal in your life.

Nail It Down: Read about God's judgment on violent behavior in Genesis 6:11-13.

99 99 99 99 99 99 99 ONE **MEDIA** 99 99 99 99 99 99 99 99

Amy Kramer, age 15. Aspiration: To become the editor-in-chief of *Vogue* magazine.

Pick a popular women's magazine and Amy—or one of her friends—subscribes to it. *Glamour, Vogue, Seventeen, Elle,* ... the girls swap them all.

Night after night they call each other to discuss new trends in the fashion industry.

"Jill, did you see that dress by Macon LeBux on page 103 of *Glamour?* I'm dying!"

"I know. I'd give anything just to wear it one night!"

Flip pages while your inside rages

Look It Up: What's the problem? Well, the more the girls look, the more they want. And the more they want, the more discontent they grow because they can't afford all those things. So they spend their days (and nights) wishing for new clothes, hating the "rotten" things they have to wear, and growing more resentful.

They need to pay attention to these words of Jesus: " 'Watch out! Be on your guard against all kinds of greed; a man's life does not consist in the abundance of his possessions' " (Luke 12:15).

Think It Through: Looking at magazines is not sinful. But realize that publishers of worldly fashion magazines (and mail order catalogs, too) have one supreme objective. Each wants to convince you that you *need* the products advertised within its pages. The ads are designed to appeal to the base elements of lust, vanity, and greed within all of us. And unfortunately, the results are very effective.

Work It Out: In the chart below, list the magazines you read regularly. Grade each one on a scale of 1-10 in the following categories (1 means it conveys a worldly outlook; 10 means it adopts a Biblical perspective):

Magazine	Image	Message
1.		
2.		
3.		
4.		

Based on your conclusions above, should you alter your reading habits? Make the commitment now to cut any negative influences out of your life.

Nail It Down: Read Ephesians 5:3.

Pray About It:

TWO

99 99 99 99 99

Our third media expert is Chris Noll, 17. Aspiration: to photograph beautiful (and scantily clad) women for a living.

He spends much of his time looking at bodies—in movies, in the *Sports Illustrated* swimsuit issue, or on the Playboy channel.

But Chris has a problem. He can't get the gorgeous bodies he's seen out of his mind—even when he wants to. Like during his algebra test. Or in church. Or when he's trying to go to sleep at night.

Keep your eyes on God, not a sexy bo

Look It Up: The human body is a beautiful creation of God. He did not intend it to be exploited in immodest display. Jesus clearly stated, " 'I tell you that anyone who looks at a woman lustfully has already committed adultery with her in his heart' " (Matthew 5:28).

Why is lust so improper for believers? Because "those who belong to Christ Jesus have crucified the sinful nature with its passions and desires" (Galatians 5:24).

Think It Through: According to both the Bible and the testimonies of those who have been controlled by lust, activities involving porno movies or skin magazines are far from harmless. Lust is an enslaving, addictive force that is *never* satisfied. It always wants more.

Media producers and ad executives fully understand this. That's why they fill their TV shows, movies, commercials, and songs with erotic images. We grow increasingly frustrated as they grow increasingly rich.

Work It Out: Quickly list what you've seen, heard, and read in the last week. Include:
- that steamy miniseries on television
- your weekend movie rentals
- radio talk shows
- MTV
- trashy romance novels and glossy skin magazines.

Are those really the kinds of images that you want to fill your mind with?

Say no to lust. Forget those destructive activities and fill your time with healthy pursuits. Find a friend who will struggle with you to keep body and mind pure in an impure world.

Nail It Down: Read Psalm 8:4-5.

THREE MEDIA

Don't dull your head with soaps

K elley Masterson, 16, is distinguished by her familiarity with soap operas. Aspiration: to direct a daytime soap.

All My Children. The Young and the Restless. The Idle and the Depraved. Kelley keeps up with them all.

Kelley's a Christian who grew up believing that abortion and divorce are wrong. But now as she watches more soaps, and spends less time in God's Word, she wonders:

"Maybe abortion is the best thing if a girl is unmarried and pregnant. I'm not sure I could stay married to the same person for life."

Look It Up: As the Israelites prepared to enter the Promised Land, God's concern was that they not become infected with pagan values. Time and again, He warned the people to live according to His Word, not according to the world:

"Be careful, or you will be enticed to turn away and worship other gods and bow down to them. . . . Fix these words of mine in your hearts and minds.

"See that you do all I command you; do not add to it or take away from it" (Deuteronomy 11:16, 18; 12:32).

Think It Through: What you see, hear, and read in the media is never free of bias. Every producer, writer, or director has some philosophy of life that colors his or her work—no matter how objective each tries to be. In fact, a study by the research team of Lichter and Rothman indicates that the most powerful figures in media are extremely antagonistic to biblical values!

Work It Out: Are you hooked on the intrigue, suspense, and excitement of the soaps? Do you love being shocked by the schemes of Erica Kane? Try something different.

Turn off your TV tonight and pick up the Bible. Read the Book of Judges. It'll take you less than an hour. There won't be any cliff-hangers. Your values won't be challenged by the denial of absolute morality. Devious men and women won't be portrayed as winners.

The Book of Judges paints a true picture of the suffering that sin causes. No exaggeration—you'll never find a soap opera as exciting or true-to-life as this book of the Bible. See for yourself!

Nail It Down: Read Romans 12:2.

Pray About It: _____

FOUR

Here's one last close-up of a member of the Pratt Academy Media Club:

Walter Waugh, 14, is a radical genius. Aspiration: to write a science fiction series and produce it into several blockbuster movies.

Walter's not very popular but what does he care? He's got his hands full reading sci-fi novels, seeing fantasy movies, and dabbling in psychic phenomena.

Yesterday he sat for a full hour staring at a piece of paper balanced on a pencil, determined to move the paper with his mind. It didn't work. But he'll keep trying.

"Confucius say, 'God is wiser!' "

Look It Up: One of the most disturbing trends in the media is the increasing attention to New Age thinking. The Bible soundly condemns this philosophy:

"See to it that no one takes you captive through hollow and deceptive philosophy, which depends on human tradition and the basic principles of this world rather than on Christ" (Colossians 2:8).

Though it claims to put people in touch with God and themselves, New Age thought is deceptive.

Think It Through: Remember the media frenzy accompanying the release of *Star Wars, Return of the Jedi* and *E.T.* ? Exciting, funny, and full of spectacular special effects, these cutting-edge films were, and still are, seen by millions of people.

But what most viewers fail to realize while watching Luke, and Obi-Wan struggle with Darth Vader is that they are also getting a crash course in Zen Buddhism.

Work It Out: The steaming hot chocolate looks delicious—until you learn that the mug also contains one drop of poison. Would you still drink it? Well, many people do just that. They get so caught up in how a movie looks ("It's so amazing! You'll laugh your head off!") that often they don't realize the dangerous messages being presented at the same time.

Be discerning when it comes to entertainment:

• Keep a sharp lookout today for the unbiblical ideas that are so common in the media.

• See if you can isolate two or three statements or ideas that are being communicated that are clearly wrong.

• Watch closely for New Age philosophy!

Nail It Down: Read Hebrews 13:9 on Saturday; on Sunday read 2 Timothy 4:3-4.

FIVE MEDIA

THE GREAT DEBATE

Teenager No. 1: "Well, I think they've sold out. They're big stars now, but only because they leave Jesus out of their songs."

Teenager No. 2: "Are you kidding? They haven't sold out! They've just sold some records to people who otherwise wouldn't buy Christian music. What's wrong with that?"

The great Christian music debate: Because of the "secular" success of some well-known Christian artists, a lot of Christian teens (and adults) have had some version of the above conversation.

And though I know you may disagree, I'm going to take sides. In my opinion, Teenager No. 2—the one defending Christian artists who do songs not explicitly about Jesus—has the better argument. Here's why:

Music is not only for evangelism: Who ever said that music has to be evangelistic to be moral? As far as I know, God hasn't. There is no Bible verse I can think of that forbids musical expression of other themes besides explicitly religious ones.

A question of perspective: Christian artists and musicians must approach their work from the perspective of truth, of course. But a truthful perspective encompasses *all* of God's creation. It's not limited to the church only.

That's why Christian architects do more than design churches. They design churches, office buildings, libraries, banks, and more—with the intent of glorifying God with their work. That's why Christian teachers teach other subjects besides theology. They teach theology, history, math, science, and physical education—with the intent of glorifying God with their work.

God created marriage. How could it be wrong for Amy Grant to sing a song celebrating her love for her husband? In the book of Ecclesiastes, Solomon tells us about the meaninglessness of life lived as if the physical universe is all that exists. How could it be wrong to sing a song reflecting on that truth (Michael W. Smith's "Place in This World?")?

Drawing the line: There is a line, of course. It is *never* moral to use art to glorify a false philosophy or to condone sinful behavior—regardless of the reason. If Amy Grant were to sing about how great premarital sex is, and then try to justify it as a way to reach promiscuous teens, she would be guilty of a terrible sin. But as long as this new breed of cross-over Christian artists are looking out on the world from the perspective of truth (Philippians 4:8), I say bravo!

That's one editor's viewpoint. Maybe you could see it that way too.

LIFE IN BIBLE TIMES

"**A** long school year, but what a recess!"

In New Testament times, only boys received a formal education outside the home. For them, school was a year-round proposition. However, during the hot summer months, classes were limited to about four hours per day with a mid-day break from ten in the morning until three in the afternoon!

"A quality alternative to TV."

It was typical for the men in the Jewish village to gather daily after the evening meal. Sitting in a large circle, the men would relate the events of the day or tell stories from ages past. Together they would sing, laugh, and swap proverbs. Older boys would stand on the edge of the circle and listen attentively.

"Please keep your knees off the table!"

In ancient Palestine, "tables" were actually circular pieces of skin or leather that were laid on the floor. These "tables" had loops around their edges and a draw-string through the loops. After each meal, the skin was brushed off, the cord was tightened, and the "table" was hung on the wall.

"You ate what?"

Rich Roman feasts (perhaps like the one mentioned in Matthew 14:6-12) included exotic appetizers like jellyfish and fungi. The main course would then feature an exquisite delicacy like flamingo tongue, wild boar, or lobster with truffles. Dessert? Pastry and fruit.

"No wonder I feel so tired!"

Most people slept on a rug or straw mat laid on the bare earthen floor. For covering they used the cloak they had worn in the day. Mattresses and pajamas were luxuries that only the wealthy and royalty enjoyed.

"Now that's what I call a wedding!"

A Jewish wedding ceremony was a festive procession in which a bridegroom would go to the home of his bride and bring her back to his home. There followed a party/feast that sometimes lasted more than one week.

FORGIVENESS
Not the Way of the World

When you're 25 or 50 or 75, you may not remember much about this magazine. But if you forget everything else, please at least try to grasp the thoughts discussed in the next few pages.

Take your time. Read carefully. Think clearly. Pray intensely. Discuss earnestly. Because the truths you are about to study have the potential to change you forever. No kidding . . . they can be the difference between an O.K. life and an incredible one.

Which one sounds better to you?

"In him we have redemption through his blood, the forgiveness of sins, in accordance with the riches of God's grace" (Ephesians 1:7).

Sins—
Feb. 15

* Copied
  Chris' test
* Gossiped
  at lunch
* Told Mrs.
  Grady a lie
  about my
  homework
* Told Mom
  that wasn't
  want
  clean
  room
* Wasn't
  consider
  of Julie's
  feelings
* Was a bad
  example at
  the game on
  Friday

At Bible study, Frances and Kirby heard this: "Because of sin, the entire human race is under a death sentence. But Jesus came and paid the penalty for sin by dying in our place. If you trust Him, you can experience total forgiveness.

"Forgiveness isn't based on anything you do to earn it. It's based on what Jesus has already done. He paid for your sins. Now the question is: Will you accept that payment?"

Frances said yes. Kirby said no, reasoning, "That can't be right! Surely, God must expect me to do something to make up for my sins."

Your debt has been paid in full

Look It Up: The book of Acts tells how the followers of Christ went all over the known world with the message of forgiveness:
- "All the prophets testify about him that everyone who believes in him receives forgiveness of sins through his name" (Acts 10:43).
- "Therefore, my brothers, I want you to know that through Jesus the forgiveness of sins is proclaimed to you" (Acts 13:38).

No wonder they were excited: Jesus completely paid the debt we could never pay!

Think It Through: You break the law and are caught. Because of your crime, the judge fines you $1,000. What are you going to do? You deserve to be punished. Yet you don't have the money to pay the penalty.

Suddenly, the judge pulls out his checkbook, and pays the fine you owe. Your debt to society has been canceled. Your offense is forgiven.

God has done that for us on an infinitely grander scale. The very payment He demanded for sin—death—He has supplied through His Son.

Work It Out: If you've already experienced forgiveness through Christ, tell God how thankful you are. Then tell someone else.

If you're not sure, you can be by sincerely praying: "God, I know I've sinned. I need and want to be forgiven. Right now, I am trusting Jesus to be my Savior. I believe the message of the Bible—that His death on the cross paid the penalty for all my sins. Amen."

Nail It Down: Read Acts 2:38.

* ✻ ✻ ✻ ✻ ✻ ONE **FORGIVENESS** ✻

Two years ago, during their sophomore year, Kirby and Frances went out for about four months. The relationship had gotten extremely physical when suddenly, for no apparent reason, Kirby stopped calling Frances.

Hurt and confused, Frances could not understand why Kirby would not return her phone calls. As she tried to work through the pain and guilt, she said, "I know that God has forgiven me for what I did. I'm just not sure that I can forgive myself."

Turn off the tape player!

Look It Up: Refusing to forgive ourselves when God says He's forgiven us makes no sense. It's like saying that we know more about dealing with sin than God does. Notice that He not only forgives, He also forgets:

• "I have swept away your offenses like a cloud, your sins like the morning mist" (Isaiah 44:22).

• "As far as the east is from the west, so far has he removed our transgressions from us" (Psalm 103:12).

• "You will tread our sins underfoot and hurl all our iniquities into the depths of the sea" (Micah 7:19).

Think It Through: Every time we really determine to walk with God or serve Him, the devil starts playing taped reruns of all our sins and whispering, "You're no good. God could never use a sinner like you."

Maybe this explains why Frances was like a spiritual yo-yo for almost a year. How should she have responded in light of God's promised forgiveness?

Work It Out: If you can't forgive yourself for certain actions, pray: "God, though You say I am totally forgiven, I realize I have never forgiven myself for _____ . Right now I choose to believe what You say, and also to forgive myself. Once and for all, I ask You to lift that burden from me and release me from my guilt."

The next time Satan brings up sins from your past, fight back with the Word of God. He will not be able to stand against you or tell you lies when you pull out your spiritual sword.

• "Who is he that condemns? Christ Jesus . . . who was raised to life . . . is also interceding for us" (Romans 8:34).

• "The one who is in you is greater than the one who is in the world" (1 John 4:4).

Nail It Down: Read Isaiah 43:25.

Pray About It:

TWO

Up until a month ago, Frances could not stand even the thought of Kirby. Though they had broken up over two years ago, she still felt angry about their whole experience. She felt used and mistreated.

To get back, she avoided Kirby at school. And any time he came to youth group activities, she ignored him. "Until he apologizes for what he did to me, I'll never even speak to him."

Four weeks ago something happened. Frances's preacher talked about forgiveness. Frances hasn't been the same since.

Forgiveness is for giving

Look It Up: The following facts prompted the change in Frances's attitude:
- God has forgiven us for all the wrong things we have done (Psalm 103:3).
- Because God has forgiven us, we must forgive others. "Bear with each other and forgive whatever grievances you may have against one another. Forgive as the Lord forgave you" (Colossians 3:13).
- Our fellowship with God is interrupted when we refuse to forgive others. "For if you forgive men when they sin against you, your heavenly Father will also forgive you. But if you do not forgive men their sins, your Father will not forgive your sins" (Matthew 6:14-15).

Think It Through: Forgiveness is not:
- denying that you've been hurt;
- explaining away the wrong behavior of someone;
- trying to understand why a person has acted a certain way.

Forgiveness is consciously choosing to release others from debts we feel they owe us because of hurts they have caused us.

Whom in your life do you need to forgive?

Work It Out: You can experience the freedom Frances found by praying:

"God, I am angry and hurt because of what _____ has done to me. I don't feel like forgiving, and in my own strength I know I can't. But because You have completely forgiven me, right now I choose to forgive _____ for _____ . Today, by Your grace, I will begin accepting _____ , and I will seek to rebuild our broken fellowship."

Nail It Down: Read Matthew 18:23-35.

✦ ✗ ✗ ✗ ✗ ✗ THREE **FORGIVENESS** ✗

When Frances understood God's forgiveness, she began her spiritual journey. Learning to forgive herself was her first obstacle, but in time she was back on track. She took another giant step by realizing the need to forgive others—especially Kirby.

The other day Frances was telling a friend some of the things she's been learning. When the subject of forgiveness came up, the friend exploded:

"God forgive *me*? If anything, I need to be forgiving Him! Why did He let my Dad die when I was only two? How could He?"

Does God need our forgiveness?

Look It Up: People understandably question God when life gets rough. King David was no exception:

"My God, my God, why have you forsaken me? Why are you so far from saving me? . . . O my God, I cry out by day, but you do not answer, by night, and am not silent" (Psalm 22:1-2).

For David, relief finally came when he remembered God's perfection and His faithfulness (Psalm 22:4-5). That's how we should respond too.

Think It Through: In his best selling book, *When Bad Things Happen to Good People*, Rabbi Harold Kushner suggests that we need to forgive God for being unable to prevent bad experiences from entering our lives.

Such an idea is blasphemous! God is perfect and needs no forgiveness—He cannot sin against us. But we live in a fallen world, where our sin has allowed disease, hatred violence, and other miseries to enter. As long as God gives us free will, we are going to be free to decide to sin . . . and to suffer the consequences.

Work It Out: If you're holding a grudge against God for letting suffering into your life, you might want to pray something like this:

"Lord, I feel angry at You because of _____ . I admit that I've been prideful and stubborn, believing that I know better than You what's best for me. Right now I give up my angry demands for an explanation. I willingly accept the circumstances You have allowed in my life. I choose to trust You. Keep reminding me that You are totally wise and completely good. Amen."

Nail It Down: See Jeremiah's anger at God—Jeremiah 20:7-18.

Pray About It:

F O U R

❋ ❋ ❋ ❋ ❋

Frances went to have lunch after church with a new girl named Jean Marie. Eventually the small talk turned into a serious conversation.

"That was really good, that stuff you said about forgiving others," the newcomer sighed. "I guess I should feel that way too . . . but there's no way." Jean Marie's eyes filled with tears. "I can never forgive my stepfather for all the wrong things he's done to me." She burst out crying, "I hate him so much! I pray every night that he'll die!"

What happens if I refuse to forgive?

Look It Up: Bitterness hurts us far more than it will ever harm anyone else. The story of Saul is a sober reminder of this fact. He became bitter because the people praised David more than they did him:

"As they danced, they sang: 'Saul has slain his thousands, and David his tens of thousands.' Saul was very angry; this refrain galled him. . . . And from that time on Saul kept a jealous eye on David" (1 Samuel 18:7-9).

From that point, Saul's life was downhill. He grew insecure, violent, and irrational. Because he never dealt with his bitterness, his life ended in ruin and disgrace.

Think It Through: One pastor has summed up the danger of an an unforgiving spirit like this: "It is like a hot coal. The longer and tighter it is held, the deeper the burn. Like a hot coal, bitterness, too, will leave a scar that even time cannot erase."

Remember, forgiveness does not mean that you must entirely forget what happened. It does not mean that you will immediately cease to feel hurt. But you must forgive your "debtors" before God can begin to heal you of that hurt.

Work It Out: No matter how deeply or how often you have suffered because of someone else, you *can* be freed from an unforgiving spirit.
- List all the ways you feel you have been wronged.
- Remember that God has forgiven you and that He expects you to forgive others.
- Confess your bitter attitude as sin (others can't make you bitter—bitterness is a choice).
- When appropriate, talk with the individual(s) involved, confess your bitter attitude, and ask forgiveness.

Nail It Down: Think about Hebrews 12:15 on Friday. On Saturday and Sunday memorize Ephesians 4:32.

✳ ✳ ✳ ✳ ✳ FIVE **FORGIVENESS** ✳

✳ ✳ ✳ ✳ ✳ ✳ ✳ STRESS ✳ ✳ ✳ ✳ ✳ ✳ ✳ ✳
Coping with the Pressures of Life

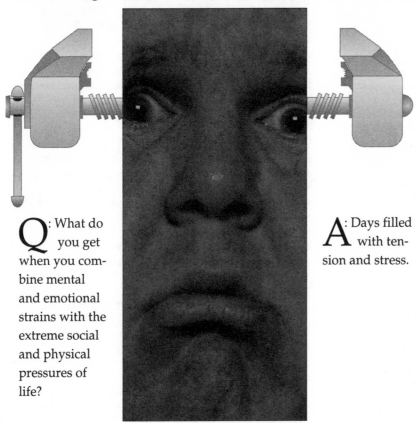

Q: What do you get when you combine mental and emotional strains with the extreme social and physical pressures of life?

A: Days filled with tension and stress.

Keep reading for biblical insight on how to cope in a pressure-packed world.

"But I call to God, and the LORD saves me. Evening, morning and noon I cry out in distress, and he hears my voice" (Psalm 55:16-17).

✳ ✳

Seventeen-year-old Adrienne is on the verge of losing it. Last year her mother suddenly left home and is living with some guy in Idaho. Now, on top of her studies, part-time job, and involvement in a couple of groups at school and church, Adrienne has the added pressure of being stand-in mom to her little sister while her dad works an extra job.

Yesterday when she got an English paper back with a big red D on it, she dissolved in tears.

"Adrienne, get a grip! It's just one paper," urged Judi.

"You don't understand!" Adrienne sobbed.

Learning to share the load

Look It Up: You don't have to live in a broken home to feel the pressure of responsibility. That kind of stress is everywhere. Consider the advice Moses got when he was worn out from settling the disputes of the people:

"What you are doing is not good.... The work is too heavy for you; you cannot handle it alone" (Exodus 18:17-18).

The speaker was Jethro, Moses' father-in-law. He urged the exhausted leader of Israel to find some helpers. "That will make your load lighter, because they will share it with you. If you do this and God so commands, you will be able to stand the strain" (vv. 22-23).

Think It Through: How can you tell when the stress levels in your life are too high? Any of the following may be warning signals: nervousness, depression, irritability, sleeping difficulty, loss of appetite (or binge eating), headaches, fatigue, frequent crying, inability to concentrate, skin problems, or apathy.

Work It Out: If you feel stressed beyond your limit, seek out others who can help lighten your load.
• Find a prayer partner during especially stressful periods.
• Look for a study buddy in your hardest class.
• Confide in a close friend during painful times.
• Pour out your heart to a parent or youth leader when you feel weary.
• Ask a brother or sister for help in completing tough tasks.

Why try to carry burdens that are too heavy for one person? The body of Christ is there to help you. But you first have to ask for help!

Nail It Down: Memorize Galatians 6:2.

✳ ✳ ✳ ✳ ✳ ✳ ONE **STRESS** ✳ ✳ ✳ ✳ ✳ ✳ ✳

L ouis Watkins is as nervous as a long-tailed cat in a room full of rocking chairs. On Saturday he takes the SAT test for the third time. His parents want him to improve his scores radically.

Each night they remind him how important it is that he study. "You need at least a 1350 or 1400, Lou!" Mr. Watkins insists (for about the 200th time). "Make us proud, son. No goofing off till after this weekend, O.K.?"

Lou nods weakly, his stomach in knots. He hates to think what will happen if he disappoints his parents.

Who's fighting your battles?

Look It Up: Have you ever battled extreme pressure? Have you ever felt so tense you wondered how you would be able to function? If so, you're not alone. Consider this charge given to Israel:

"When you go to war against your enemies . . . do not be afraid. . . . Do not be fainthearted or afraid; do not be terrified or give way to panic before them. For the LORD your God is the one who goes with you to fight for you against your enemies to give you victory" (Deuteronomy 20:1, 3-4).

What a promise! The pressure for success isn't on you. It's on God. Your obligation is simply to "go to war." It's up to God to give you the victory.

Think It Through: How would you handle the stress if you had parents like Lou? Is it right for parents to put that much pressure on their children? Is it right for us to put that much pressure on ourselves?

Work It Out: Don't lose the biblical perspective. When your back is to the wall, all you have to do is your part. What is your part in the stresses you face?
- In academics, your part is to study.
- In a conflict involving a relationship, your part is to apologize and be kind.
- In athletics, your part is to be in shape.
- In a tempting situation, your part is to turn away from sin.
- In a pressure-filled job, your part is to work hard and be cheerful.

Once you know your part, simply do your part. Then give the pressure to God. He can handle it. (He can also bring victory . . . when we trust Him.)

Nail It Down: Read Isaiah 63:7-9.

Pray About It:

✳ ✳ ✳ ✳ ✳ TWO

What would you feel like doing in the following situations?

- Biff Hooper, the biggest senior on the football team, has vowed to beat the you-know-what out of Tommy for giving his girlfriend a ride home.

- Carla Maddox has been wrongly accused of cheating during a history exam.

- Melinda just learned that her father is being transferred. She'll be moving away from the town she's lived in all her life.

- David Pearce, who has a mortal fear of speaking to large groups, has to give an oral report in class tomorrow.

Talk to God during stress's mess

Look It Up: No matter what you're facing, remember the stressful experience of David in Psalm 18:

First, David prayed. "In my distress I called to the LORD; I cried to my God for help" (v. 6).

Second, God answered. "From his temple he heard my voice; my cry came before him, into his ears" (v. 6).

Turning to God was David's immediate response. On the heels of another tense occasion, David proclaimed: "Surely God is my help; the Lord is the one who sustains me. . . . For he has delivered me from all my troubles" (Psalm 54:4, 7).

Think It Through: The words to an old hymn underscore the truth that prayer is the best response to stress:

I must tell Jesus all of my trials.
I cannot bear these burdens alone
In my distress He kindly will save me.
He always loves and cares for His own.

That one little stanza contains a lot of truth, doesn't it?

Work It Out: Some people, when facing a stressful situation, do everything but pray. They toss and turn, agonize, plan, scheme, fret, connive, plot, consult friends, worry, calculate, and finally trust in their own abilities to overcome the pressure. Why not just turn all the headaches over to God—right off the bat?

Here's what we're talking about: "Lord, I feel really stressed out because of _____ . I don't know what to do. I'm tired and scared. The problem is too big for me to handle. Please take control of the situation. Give me Your peace. Keep reminding me that You will take care of things. Amen."

Nail It Down: Read Psalm 4:1.

❋ ❋ ❋ ❋ ❋ THREE STRESS ❋ ❋ ❋ ❋ ❋ ❋ ❋

Remember Melinda? The girl who had to move from her home town? Well, nine months later, she's finally beginning to see that the situation may not be so horrible after all. She comments: "The move was so hard. We were all totally depressed at first. But what could we do? We had to lean on each other —and especially on God.

"I still miss my friends. But I'm meeting some great people at my new school and actually starting to like this place. My family is closer, and God is a bigger part of our lives now."

* * * * *

Stress can result in the best

Look It Up: It's important to remember that since God is in control, stressful circumstances can have positive results. For example, stress can:
- bring about real character in our lives: "When he has tested me, I will come forth as gold" (Job 23:10);
- cause us to have a closer walk with Christ (2 Corinthians 12:7-10);
- provide opportunities for us to be good examples to others: "In spite of severe suffering, you welcomed the message with the joy given by the Holy Spirit. And so you became a model to all the believers in Macedonia and Achaia" (1 Thessalonians 1:6-7);
- result in future reward: "For our light and momentary troubles are achieving for us an eternal glory that far outweighs them all" (2 Corinthians 4:17).

Think It Through: Consider how hard times produce character. Do you turn to Christ when the pressures rise in your life? In your most recent stressful situation, how good an example were you to others? God really does give future glory for those who patiently endure present difficulties.

Work It Out: If you find yourself cornered by stress right now, stop focusing on your negative circumstances. Try these three steps:
1. Ask God to show you the positive aspects of your situation. There are always *some*.
2. Memorize one of the verses cited in today's "Look It Up" section.
3. Quote that verse to yourself every time you are tempted to forget that God is in control of the stress in your life.

Nail It Down: Read Romans 8:28.

Pray About It: —————————————

FOUR

L ast week was full of stress for Helen Williams.

On Monday she waited to receive her term paper. She had put off the assignment until the night before it was due. The grade wouldn't be good.

On Wednesday Helen dreaded bumping into Martha Porter. Why? Basically, Helen had made a rude remark about Martha, Martha found out, and Helen feared a showdown.

Friday night, at a party, Helen yielded to the influence of friends who were saying, "Have a drink—loosen up!" Later that same night in the car, Rob pressured Helen with a similar message.

Avoiding needless pressures

Look It Up: Have you ever considered that many of the stresses we face, we really bring on ourselves? Such pressures can be avoided by following two biblical principles:

1. Alter your lifestyle and become more disciplined. "Be very careful, then, how you live—not as unwise but as wise, making the most of every opportunity, because the days are evil" (Ephesians 5:15-16).

2. Avoid certain situations altogether—"Flee the evil desires of youth, and pursue righteousness, faith, love and peace, along with those who call on the Lord out of a pure heart" (2 Timothy 2:22).

Think It Through: What, if anything, could Helen have done to eliminate the stresses she felt regarding the term paper? The Martha Porter incident? The temptations she faced on Friday night?

What can you learn from her mistakes to avoid having to go through similar stresses yourself?

Work It Out: Eliminate some future stress today by doing one or more of the following:

• Begin working ahead on a big school assignment. Do some advance research for an upcoming paper or start reading that big novel for English.

• Bite your tongue when tempted to say something negative about someone. (Such comments almost always come back to haunt us and create tension in our relationships.)

• Refuse invitations to go places where you know you'll face incredible peer pressure.

Nail It Down: Read Psalm 20:1-4. On Saturday read the rest of Psalm 20. On Sunday read 2 Chronicles 20:1-30.

✳ ✳ ✳ ✳ ✳ FIVE STRESS ✳ ✳ ✳ ✳ ✳ ✳ ✳

SUICIDE

Nah. It couldn't happen to them. Dad is a godly man. Mom embodies the Proverbs 31 woman. The children are good students and active in the church youth groups. Suicide couldn't possibly happen to a family like that, right? Wrong. Rich, poor, Christian, non-Christian—all kinds of kids take their lives. And that's a colossal tragedy.

The ugly truth: About one-third of American teenagers have contemplated taking their own lives.

Almost 10,000 teen suicides are reported annually, which makes it a leading cause of death among young people. Some experts say that the actual number of teen suicides is twice the reported figure because many teen suicides are wrongly reported as accidents.

The ugly reasons: Why would young people, who are just starting out in life, decide to end their own lives? Kids who have attempted suicide cite a variety of reasons:

• They were under too much pressure at school or at home.

• Their own drug and/or alcohol abuse.

• They wanted to escape an abusive parent.

• Overpowering feeling that life isn't worth the trouble.

The beautiful solution: There is an answer to the despair that causes teens to make the fateful, fatal decision to kill. The answer is that in Jesus Christ, God has forgiven your sins. The pressure is off.

Sure, God wants you to do the best you can with the talents He's given you. But that's all He expects. He doesn't expect you to be a totally together, mythical superperson. He accepts you, flaws and all.

The bottom line: If you are feeling extremely withdrawn and depressed—or if thoughts of suicide are in your mind constantly—don't ignore the problem, get help. Talk about your feelings with someone honestly and openly. Destroying the life God gave you is despising His most precious gift. Your negative feelings may not seem temporary, but hang on. Help is available so that you can face your problems and go forward to enjoy life.

CARPE DIEM

Say *what?* Before we explain that title, think about this: Most people will spend *today* looking forward to *tomorrow.* Unable to find fulfillment and contentment in the *now*, they will daydream about the *later.* That's why we constantly hear statements like: "I can't wait till this weekend!" or "Things will be so great when we're finally seniors!" or "Once I get my license, my life will be perfect!" The focus is always on the future.

Do you think the people who live this way—thinking mainly about tomorrow—are truly satisfied when tomorrow arrives? Not likely. Chances are they end up wasting *that* new day looking ahead to the next!

There are at least two problems with this futuristic obsession:

1. It shields us from what really is (reality) by filling our minds with what might be (fantasy). The result is sad—we miss out on the wonder of life all around us.

2. It involves speculation and guesswork. No one (except God) can know what the future holds (James 4:13-16).

So, how do we get out of the "tomorrow rut?" By coming to know the Creator of all our yesterdays, todays, and tomorrows. When we enter into a relationship with God by trusting in His Son, Jesus Christ, we understand first hand what King David meant when he said, *"My times are in your hands"* (Psalm 31:15). Only then are we able to live out the words of Jesus, *"Do not worry about tomorrow, for tomorrow will worry about itself"* (Matthew 6:34).

Now, about "carpe diem." That's Latin for "seize the day." It means live for today, not tomorrow. If you have never trusted Christ to forgive your sins, seize the day (and eternal life) by believing in Him (John 5:24). If you already know Christ, seize the day by living totally for Him (John 10:10).

Go ahead—seize the day!

PROM
A Tale of Two Siblings

Charles Dickens might have described it this way:
"It was the best of proms. It was the worst of proms."
Best for Rebecca, 18-year-old senior. Worst for Patrick, her
17-year-old brother. Want to find out the details?

*"Dear friends, I urge you, as aliens and strangers in the world, to
abstain from sinful desires, which war against your soul. Live such good
lives among the pagans that, though they accuse you of doing wrong,
they may see your good deeds and glorify God on the day he visits us"*
(1 Peter 2:11-12).

Only six weeks until the party of the year. Not much time to plan—but more than enough time for bad attitudes to develop.

• Rebecca spent four long weeks anxiously wondering if she'd get asked to the prom. When no calls came, she felt worthless.

• Patrick thought of all the ways he, Cal, and Mark could become Henderson High legends with the most exotic and outrageous prom dates ever!

In the junior and senior classes, the competition for dates was fierce. Rumors were flying, friendships were strained by envy, and the back-stabbing was at an all-time high.

The provocative promise of prom

Look It Up: The prospect of the prom can do strange things to people! In all the excitement and pressure to out-do classmates, Christians can get their priorities twisted and their attitudes mixed up. When that happens, it's always helpful to remember God's truth.

"For the grace of God that brings salvation has appeared to all men. It teaches us to say 'No' to ungodliness and worldly passions, and to live self-controlled, upright and godly lives in this present age" (Titus 2:11-12).

Think It Through: Christians can defeat the harmful attitudes that often accompany the prom. Feelings of worthlessness, competition, jealousy, and bitterness don't have to dominate your life.

Think about how Jesus lived. He was totally given over to God's will; He had peace of mind and spirit at all times, without isolating Himself from what was going on around Him. God's grace can free you up to enjoy life, not envy others.

What kind of attitudes fill your mind when prom season rolls around?

Work It Out: List the attitudes your friends project when planning for the prom. How do they compare with the two sets of standards in Galatians 5:19-26?

Rate yourself using the same passage. Are your goals and desires at prom time fleshly or spiritual? Spend some time thinking about this portion of Scripture. (And if you really want to get a grip on the right prom attitude, take time out to memorize those wise words from the pen of the apostle Paul.)

Nail It Down: Read James 3:14-16.

❖ ❖ ❖ ❖ ❖ ❖ **ONE PROM** ❖ ❖ ❖ ❖ ❖ ❖ ❖

In his quest to wow everyone at the prom, Patrick has run up quite a bill: Tuxedo rental, $75; flowers, $65; one-third of a three-hour limousine rental, $60; dinner for two at Antoine's, $100. Where is Patrick getting $300? He's taking it out of his college savings — wait till his parents find out!

His date, Elaine, has shelled out a bundle too: $160 for a black velvet dress; $28 for earrings; $15 for gloves; $5 for pantyhose; $40 for shoes—not to mention $100 for a haircut and perm. Her total bill? $348.

Prom's pride packs a price

Look It Up: Does God have anything to say about the prom practice of trying to impress everyone by spending megabucks? Consider this passage:

"Do not love the world or anything in the world. If anyone loves the world, the love of the Father is not in him. For everything in the world—the cravings of sinful man, the lust of his eyes and the boasting of what he has and does—comes not from the Father but from the world. The world and its desires pass away, but the man who does the will of God lives forever" (1 John 2:15-17).

Think It Through: Here are some other points to ponder before going into debt over the prom:
• Since God is the ultimate owner of all that we possess, how much say should He have in our prom spending decisions?
• Could a couple spend less than $50 and still have fun? Why not?
• What are some creative ways you could spend less at a traditionally expensive formal event like a prom or a spring banquet?

Work It Out: Conduct a survey among your friends at school. Ask each one how much he or she plans to spend on this year's formal party.

You will probably feel the pressure to join the crowd in the prom-frenzy, or feel sorry for yourself if your parents can't afford to spend as much. Don't give in!

Pray: "God, please help me to be responsible with the possessions and finances you have given me. Show me how to be a good steward. Keep me from falling into the trap of getting into a spending competition at prom time. Amen."

Nail It Down: Read Matthew 13:22.

Pray About It: ───────────────────────────

❖ ❖ ❖ ❖ ❖ TWO

So far, Patrick's pride has cost him $300. And now his buddies are trying to get him to chip in on a deluxe hotel suite for an after-prom party. That could cost him another $75!

But enough about the money. Patrick's worried that his parents might find out. Besides, he knows how wild things could get in a hotel room with his "ready-to-party" friends.

"C'mon, Pat," urges Cal. "It'll be great. The place has a separate bedroom . . . and a hot tub!"

"Yeah, we can't afford it unless you go in with us," Mark adds.

Peer pressure vs. purity at the prom

Look It Up: Patrick feels pulled in about a hundred directions. He wants to have fun, but without things getting too crazy. He doesn't want to be a geek, but he also doesn't want to get in trouble. Something inside is telling him, "Go for it, Patrick! This is prom night!" Another voice says, "No, man, this is wrong."

Maybe Patrick needs to call time out, clear his head, and remember this command of the Lord: "Test everything. Hold on to the good. Avoid every kind of evil" (1 Thessalonians 5:21-22).

Think It Through: Couldn't Patrick go to the hotel as long as he didn't actually do anything wrong? What would be the harm in that?

1. He would be running toward (instead of away from) a very tempting situation. And that's dangerous (1 Corinthians 10:13; 2 Timothy 2:22).

2. 1 Thessalonians 5:22 has also been translated (King James Version), "Abstain from all appearance of evil." In other words, any activity that even looks questionable is out of bounds for believers.

Work It Out: Does any aspect of your prom agenda contain the appearance of evil? Based on the command above, how will you change your plan?

Decide in advance how you will handle the following situations (whether at the prom or any other party):

• Friends invite you to a hotel room where they plan to party all night.

• Your date suggests leaving early in order to go to his or her house where no one will be home all night.

• Your friends go on a drinking binge or ask you to chip in money to buy drinks.

Nail It Down: Read 1 Thessalonians 5:6.

❖ ❖ ❖ ❖ ❖ ❖ **THREE PROM** ❖ ❖ ❖ ❖ ❖ ❖ ❖ ❖

When we last saw Rebecca (Day 1), she didn't have an invitation to the prom. But rather than feel sorry for herself, she got together with friends in the same boat. With their parents, the girls planned a gigantic luau in the social hall at Rebecca's church.

What a success! About 50 people showed up, and for $15 apiece they enjoyed Polynesian decorations, great food, and Christian music videos on a big screen. A photographer was on hand. Later that night, a bus took everyone across town for a midnight bonfire overlooking Lake Henderson.

Problem proms: how to fight back

Look It Up: Ponder this passage:
"His divine power has given us everything we need for life and godliness through our knowledge of him who called us by his own glory and goodness. Through these he has given us his very great and precious promises, so that through them you may participate in the divine nature and escape the corruption in the world caused by evil desires" (2 Peter 1:3-4).

You may not believe this, but you can survive not going to the prom. How? By realizing that God has provided everything you really need for a full life.

Think It Through: Is it wrong to go to big social events like the prom? Not if you guard your attitudes and spending habits, and avoid bad situations.

Remember also that the prom isn't the only game in town. There are other, less-expensive alternatives that can be just as much fun, and a whole lot more honoring to God.

Work It Out: Tired of all the fuss over the prom? Tired of seeing everyone make such a big deal? Why not sponsor your own alternative?

Reach out to all your classmates who: don't have dates, can't afford to spend big bucks, normally get left out of the big social scene at school. Create an original theme for the party, complete with invitations, decorations, food, or even costumes.

Involve everyone, be creative, and plan an event that will be first-class and tons of fun. (And let us know what happens!)

Nail It Down: Read 1 Corinthians 10:31.

Pray About It:

❖ ❖ ❖ ❖ ❖   **FOUR**

39

Let's take one last look at prom night.

Rebecca had a blast at her luau. And today she feels great inside knowing so many other non-prom goers also had fun.

Patrick, however, had a nightmare. Some couples crashed their private party at the hotel and trashed the room. The hotel manager ended up kicking them out.

"I thought we were going to have so much fun," says Patrick sadly.

"'This is it for senior prom! It was just a big headache and a major waste of cash. I don't care if I'm the only person in school not going next year. No way I'll ever do that again!'"

When prom is a bomb

Look It Up: Everyone wants to feel accepted and important. We all want fulfillment, satisfaction, and a sense of purpose in life. And there's nothing wrong with those desires. The disappointments come when we try to fulfill those longings outside of Christ.

"For in Christ all the fullness of the Deity lives in bodily form, and you have been given fullness in Christ" (Colossians 2:9-10).

Elsewhere Paul says the same thing: a rich, meaningful life is found—not in proms, clothes, dates, limousines, or good looks—but in Christ. "For to me, to live is Christ and to die is gain" (Philippians 1:21).

Think It Through: When are Christians going to realize that they can't be happy chasing after the best of both worlds? When are we going to quit seeking those things that can never satisfy?

Jesus really is the answer to our deepest needs. But some Christians still seem to be searching.

Work It Out: Discuss the following questions with a Christian friend today:

• Is your true motivation at the prom (or other social events) to get a date and be seen, or to glorify Christ by what you say and do?

• Do you spend as much time thinking about your walk with Christ as you do over whom you will call or what you will wear to the prom?

• Which lasts longer—the satisfaction of knowing you've obeyed Christ, or the blur of a gigantic party?

• What are some ways you could participate in the prom and still maintain your Christian witness?

Nail It Down: Read Philippians 2:12-16 on Saturday and Ephesians 5:8-18 on Sunday.

❖ ❖ ❖ ❖ ❖ ❖ FIVE **PROM** ❖ ❖ ❖ ❖ ❖ ❖ ❖

•••••• CLOTHES ••••••
Taking a Peek at God's View of Chic

When it comes to clothes, how would you describe your attitude? Are you:

Satisfied ("11 pairs of jeans is enough.")

Greedy ("I want more shoes than Imelda Marcos.")

Guilty ("Must I have a different sweater for each day of the month?")

Indifferent ("Being in style is not a priority for me.")

Jealous ("I hate anyone with great clothes.")

What does God think about clothes?

"Clothe yourselves with the Lord Jesus Christ" (Romans 13:14).

It's Sunday afternoon and Lisa is looking in her closet in despair.

This morning she visited a friend's church where all the girls were wearing designer suits or Laura Ashley dresses. There sat Lisa in her skirt and sweater from Judy's Bargain Closet. She felt like everyone was staring at her and whispering.

Lisa feels sorry for herself. "It's not fair! How come I can't have nicer clothes? I have to wear these 2,000-year-old rags. I swear, my life would be 1000% better if I could dress like they do!"

Do you dress to impress?

Look It Up: Does what you wear impress God? Does He give approval only to those who wear the "right" brands? You be the judge:

• Some people with nice clothes may be destined for trouble: "There was a rich man who was dressed in purple and fine linen.... The rich man ... died and was buried. In hell, where he was in torment, he looked up" (Luke 16:19, 22-23).

• We won't be taking our favorite outfits into eternity with us: "Naked I came from my mother's womb, and naked I will depart" (Job 1:21).

Think It Through: How do you feel about these statements?

• Fashion models and designers live happy, problem-free lives because they can wear anything they want.

• Buy a whole new wardrobe for a rapist or drug addict, and he or she will be a new person.

• It's better to spend $50 a month on new clothes than $15 dollars a month to feed a child in Africa.

Work It Out: Feeling like Lisa? Take some radical steps:

• Stay out of the malls for a couple of weeks. Hanging out there will only intensify the feeling that everyone but you can afford all the clothes they want.

• Box up your *Seventeen, Sassy, Mademoiselle,* and *Elle* magazines for the time being. The ads and articles in those magazines are designed to convince you to think: "If I want to be 'in,' I need to look and dress like those models."

• Focus on what you do have instead of what you don't. Develop an attitude of thankfulness. Think of all the people in the world who have one outfit ... or less!

Nail It Down: Read James 2:1-5.

ONE **CLOTHES**

42

Lindsay, a great-looking 16 year-old, and her handsome senior boyfriend have been chosen to appear in a fashion show at the mall.

During the show Lindsay carefully arranges her face in a sultry pout —just like the models she sees in *Cosmopolitan*. When she notices several guys from school checking her out, she thinks, "I look pretty hot!"

Meanwhile when a gorgeous college student starts making eyes at Davis, he gets about as puffed up as a blowfish.

In the car on the way home, Lindsay and Davis rave about how great it is to be admired and envied.

Pride and idolatry in the closet

Look It Up: Look out! Don't let clothes make you an ego-maniac. Notice what happened when the women of Israel got haughty about their appearance:

"In that day the Lord will snatch away their finery . . . the fine robes and the capes and cloaks, the purses and mirrors, and the linen garments and tiaras and shawls. Instead of fragrance there will be a stench; instead of a sash, a rope; instead of well-dressed hair, baldness; instead of fine clothing, sackcloth; instead of beauty, branding" (Isaiah 3:18, 22-24).

Think It Through: There is nothing wrong with wanting to to look your best, showing good taste, or enjoying nice clothes. It's fun to express yourself with clothing and develop your own sense of style.

Your *attitude* about clothes is what matters. Ask yourself these questions:
• Do I think about clothes most of the time?
• Does what I have on make me feel important?
• Do I appraise others strictly by what they wear?
• Do all my friends dress exactly the same way?

Work It Out: If you place too much emphasis on clothes or are overly concerned about your wardrobe, pray this:

"God, my attitude about fashion is messed up. I have allowed what I wear to become too important. I'm sorry. Show me how You view clothes. And then help me to get that same perspective this week. Amen."

An experiment for the brave: Wear something really tacky and out-of-style to youth group this week. Ask each member to give his or her reaction. It's a great way to open up a discussion on the importance of clothing!

Nail It Down: Read Matthew 23:27.

Pray About It:

TWO

I t looked more like a fashion show at Fredrick's of Hollywood than it did a youth missions trip to the beach.

Some of the girls were wearing teeny string bikinis. When Rick, the youth director, told them to "put some clothes on!" they put on t-shirts which soon became thoroughly wet.

A few of the guys weren't much better. They paraded around in their Spandex racing suits until Rick's wife complained, "C'mon guys! Please put some real swimsuits on."

Modesty is our policy

Look It Up: The Bible does have something to say about those Christians who make it a habit of running around in seductive clothing:

"I also want women to dress modestly, with decency and propriety, not with braided hair or gold or pearls or expensive clothes, but with good deeds, appropriate for women who profess to worship God" (1 Timothy 2:9).

This verse is addressed to females, but guys need to pay attention as well. If we claim to follow and worship Christ, it is hypocritical to send out sexual messages by the way we dress.

Think It Through: Girls, if you could read a guy's mind when you wear revealing clothes, you'd never wear those outfits again. Do you want to be thought of as an impersonal sex object, lusted over like a piece of meat? Then don't dress like a tramp.

If Christians really care about each other (and God commands us to), we must be willing to stop doing anything and everything that causes a brother or sister in Christ to have wrong thoughts. That includes wearing certain clothes.

Work It Out: Are we saying that Christians should dress in ugly, bulky burlap? No! But we are saying that indecent dress is out-of-bounds for believers.

Take a bold step. Girls, ask a mature Christian lady (guys should ask a man) to help you go through your wardrobe and weed out whatever is improper. We're not just talking about swimwear (fashions can be immodest at places other than the beach). What about those tight jeans and sweaters, low-cut dresses, miniskirts that are too short and tight tank tops, off-the-shoulder sweatshirts, half T-shirts, etc.?

Nail It Down: Read Proverbs 11:22.

• • • • • • • THREE **CLOTHES** • • • •

Remember Lisa? The girl who felt angry because the girls at her friend's church have ritzy clothes? Well, today she feels nervous because she's been invited by some of those girls to a party this weekend.

Her stomach is in knots. "What in the world can I wear?" she asks. "Nothing I have is right! Maybe I could borrow some money from Uncle Frank and go to the mall tonight. I'd rather die than look out of place with those girls."

Dressed up, stressed out

Look It Up: Jesus has a wise word for anxious Lisa (and for everyone else who gets uptight about clothes):

" 'And why do you worry about clothes? See how the lilies of the field grow. They do not labor or spin. Yet I tell you that not even Solomon in all his splendor was dressed like one of these. If that is how God clothes the grass of the field, which is here today and tomorrow is thrown into the fire, will he not much more clothe you, O you of little faith?' " (Matthew 6:28–33).

Think It Through: Azalea bushes don't get stressed out about what they look like. They just do what they were created to do—grow and blossom, giving glory to God (Isaiah 44:23).

In the same way our responsibility is simply to do what we were created to do without comparing ourselves to others—seek first God's kingdom and His righteousness. As we do that God will provide the clothing we need. The real beauty that grows as a flower of love and obedience far outshines anything we can put on our bodies. (More about that tomorrow.)

Work It Out: If your constant concern is clothing, not Christ, do these things:

1. The next time you feel an impulse to go out and buy a new outfit, ask yourself whether you really need it.

2. Do not feel sorry for yourself because of clothes you don't have.

3. Stubbornly resist envy of anyone. Remember the Tenth Commandment.

4. Pray about your anxious attitude: "Father, do whatever it takes to cause me to see that clothes are just not worth worrying about. Amen."

Nail It Down: Read 1 Timothy 6:8.

Pray About It:

•••• FOUR

45

You probably have people like Kay and Kent at your school. She's beautiful. He's gorgeous. Since their mother is a buyer for a big department store, they each have a closet full of great clothes. They are voted "Most Beautiful" and "Most Handsome" year after year.

But the problem is that Kay and Kent know they're good-looking and they let you know it. Hang around them for just a few minutes and their conceited, stuck-up, arrogant personalities will get on your nerves really quick.

The well-dressed soul

Look It Up: Suzanne is a bit overweight and she gets her clothes at an outlet store. Yet she's 50 times more popular than Kay. Why are people attracted to her? Because she's fun and interesting and cares about people.

"Your beauty should not come from outward adornment, such as braided hair and the wearing of gold jewelry and fine clothes. Instead, it should be that of your inner self, the unfading beauty of a gentle and quiet spirit, which is of great worth in God's sight" (1 Peter 3:3-4).

Real character will improve your appearance more than the hottest, most expensive fashions in *GQ* or *Glamour*. (And it never goes out of style!)

Think It Through: Having a perfect wardrobe and wearing the right clothes will not solve all your problems and make your life perfect. The best-dressed people in your class still fight with their parents, argue with friends, and break up with boyfriends and girlfriends. The real difficulties in your life do not come from a flawed fashion-sense, but a flawed character.

Work It Out: Quit focusing so much on outer appearance and concentrate instead on dressing up your character. Some practical help:

• When you get dressed each morning, don't forget to put on Christ (Romans 13:14). To clothe yourself in Him means you let others see Him at work in your life.

• As you put on your shoes today, tell God that you'll go wherever He sends you.

• If it's still cold where you live, put on your gloves and commit your hands to the Lord's service.

Nail It Down: Read Colossians 3:12 on Saturday and 1 Peter 5:5 on Sunday.

• • • • • • • FIVE **CLOTHES** • • • •

FOOD
Eating to Live ... or Living to Eat?

"So whether you eat or drink or whatever you do, do it all for the glory of God" (1 Corinthians 10:31).

Few things so consistently control our thoughts and lives. From the womb to the tomb, from business brunches to dinner dates, from the kitchen cabinet to the couch, almost everything we do is centered around food. We spend billions of dollars munching out ... and then billions more shaping up ... so that we can munch out again!

Such an obsession raises a lot of questions. Not surprisingly, the Bible gives us a lot of good "food for thought."

47

Marti Cason fantasizes about a huge hot fudge sundae with whipped cream. At 5' 6" and 113 pounds, Marti could afford to indulge herself once in awhile. But Marti doesn't eat much of anything. She's terrified of gaining weight.

Mrs. Cason worries that Marti is getting too thin. She tries to entice her with her favorite meals, but Marti just picks at her food. During her morning and evening workouts she tells herself: "Just ten more pounds, and I'll be perfect."

Ten more pounds, and Marti might be dead.

Refusing food or losing food

Look It Up: Anorexia nervosa is a serious eating disorder most common in young women. Medical facts tell us that self-starvation is wrong—and so does the Bible:

• Obsession with one's body image is not a desirable character trait. Your appearance matters very little to God (1 Samuel 16:7). Should you focus on something that is relatively unimportant to Him?

• Your body is to be treated with respect: "Do you not know that your body is a temple of the Holy Spirit?" (1 Corinthians 6:19). Self-starvation is abuse of the body.

• Your worth is not dependent on an ideal body. You are priceless in God's eyes (1 John 3:1), "wonderfully made" (Psalm 139:14) and loved by Him.

Think It Through: Do you crave food but refuse to eat because you're afraid of getting fat? Do you feel panicky or angry when others try to persuade you to eat?

If so, you may be in danger of developing anorexia nervosa. If allowed to progress, it will lead to emaciation, hair loss, cessation of menstrual periods—and ultimately to heart failure and death. Self-starvation is definitely *not* a way to achieve physical beauty.

Work It Out: If you identify with the behavior and tendencies described above:

1. Acknowledge that you have a problem. Confess your feelings about food to God; ask for His help.

2. Share your secret today with a mature Christian that you trust. Ask him or her to help you find help. That step could be a major turning point in your life.

3. As you read this week's topic, make a list of Bible verses that help you transform your thinking regarding food, looks, and your self-worth.

Nail It Down: Read Romans 12:1-2.

ONE FOOD

Kathryn often gives Marti a ride home from school. After dropping her off, Kathryn stops to buy a half-gallon of ice cream, an apple pie, and six candy bars. When she gets home, she quietly takes the food to her room and eats it—all of it. Then she calmly goes to the bathroom and vomits. She feels serene, cleansed.

No one would guess that Kathryn eats like this three times a week. Kathryn thinks her binge/purge habit is harmless. But, just like Marti, she is slowly destroying her body.

The roller coaster of eating disorder

Look It Up: Kathryn's eating disorder, as you may know, is called *bulimia*. People who are bulimic stuff down huge quantities of food, then induce vomiting or use laxatives to "purge" their system. This cycle is not only harmful to the body; there are spiritual consequences as well.

• Gluttony is sin—rebellion against God's design for food. Although bulimics may not keep the food in their bodies, the act of eating uncontrollably is sinful. "The fruit of the Spirit is . . . self control" (Galations 5:22-23).

• As Christians, we are to be controlled by the Holy Spirit—not by compulsive-obsessive behavior: "Therefore do not let sin reign in your mortal body so that you obey its evil desires" (Romans 6:12).

Think It Through: It doesn't take a genius to figure out that if you don't allow food to stay in your body, you're not going to get the nutrients you need from it.

Here's what bulimics can expect over the long term: malnutrition, depression, injury to the esophagus and stomach, severe rectal bleeding, erosion of tooth enamel leading to tooth loss, heart damage, and numerous other complications. Is being ultra-thin worth all that?

Work It Out: If you are in the grip of bulimia, or if you struggle with bulimic tendencies, you need to stop denying the problem *today*. If you've tried to stop in the past and failed, don't despair. You *can* get help.

First, talk to God about what you've been doing (He already knows) and tell Him that you want to be helped. Then go back to yesterday's Work it Out section and follow those steps.

Nail It Down: Read Romans 6:11-17.

Pray About It: ─────────────────────────

 T W O

"I'd give anything to be her," Kathryn thinks as Marti gets out of the car. "I'm just a fat slob." Overcome with self-pity, Kathryn turns into a fast food drive-thru.

Meanwhile Marti stands in front of the mirror, looking at herself in disgust.
"I can't believe I scarfed that pizza today." (She had one piece.) Brian is going to absolutely freak if I don't get rid of these thighs." (Actually, Brian thinks Marti would look better with a few more pounds.) "If I could just look as good as Kathryn" (Marti weighs 20 pounds less than Kathryn).

Are you grateful for your grub?

Look It Up: People with eating disorders are often somewhat out of touch with reality—usually the reality about themselves. The food fixation is only a symptom of something deeper that is troubling them. If only Kathryn and Marti would turn to God instead of food:
- "Then Jesus declared, 'I am the bread of life. He who comes to me will never go hungry, and he who believes in me will never be thirsty' " (John 6:35).
- "You open your hand and satisfy the desires of every living thing" (Psalm 145:16).
- "The LORD is close to the brokenhearted and saves those who are crushed in spirit" (Psalm 34:18).

Think It Through: Do you think more about what you will or will not *eat* than what you will *do?* Do you ever eat because you feel lonely, depressed, or angry? Do you feel that you are not worthy to be loved exactly as you are?

No matter how you feel about yourself, God couldn't love you more. He wants to heal whatever hurts you have; He wants to fill the empty place in you with Himself. And He wants you to be free. That's why He sent His Son Jesus—to set us free from the things that control us and keep us apart from Him.

Work It Out: If you recognize yourself (even a little) in Marti or Kathryn, pray this prayer in your own words: "Father, my problem with food is controlling my life. I know I'm hurting myself but I don't know how to stop. I want to be free from my eating disorder—I want You to be in control. Please lead me to the right place for help."

Then seek Christian counseling. If your church does not provide it, ask your pastor to refer you to a counselor.

Nail It Down: Read Psalm 34 aloud, and Galatians 5:1.

THREE FOOD

L ast week both Marti and Kathryn had to face the seriousness of their problems when Marti passed out in class and the doctor found out that she hadn't eaten at all in three days.

Kathryn couldn't hide her problem when she started vomiting involuntarily after a meal. She didn't have to force herself; the food just came up by itself.

Now both girls are getting medical care and family counseling. One of the many things they will have to work through is their perspective of food—what it is, and what it is not.

Gluttons pop their buttons!

Look It Up: Every human being is born with the instinct to eat. When God first created Adam and Eve, He gave them (1) each other; (2) dominion over the earth; and (3) food (Genesis 1:28-29). He also gave us the ability to enjoy eating. (Think about it—God *could* have given us bodies that lived on oxygen alone.)

But as a society we tend to get carried away with the importance of food; we're either diet-crazed, fiber-obsessed, or victims of Big Mac Attacks. Jesus has good words to offer to every culture about food: "Do not worry about your life, what you will eat or drink; . . . Is not life more important than food?" (Matthew 6:25).

Think It Through: When you get right down to it, what is food? The media will try to tell you it's the "Real Thing," or the "Right Thing to Do," or even that "Snickers Satisfies You," but what is food, really?

Food is fuel. That's it. Food provides what you need so that your body can develop and function properly. Someone like Marti might see food as an enemy, while Kathryn sees food as a comforter and means of control. But food was not given to us for those purposes.

Work It Out: Using a concordance, try to find as many biblical references to food as you can.
• What kinds of things are expressed by people eating together in the Bible?
• What commands did God give the Jews regarding their diet? (Hint: Check out Leviticus.)
• Identify some of the foods that were popular then and compare them to your favorite "delicacies."

Nail It Down: Read Deuteronomy 8:3 and John 6:51.

Pray About It:

FOUR

◄◄ ◄◄ ◄◄ ◄◄ ◄◄

Marti and Kathryn aren't the only people in the cafeteria with poor eating habits.

There's Ashton, getting a diet soda to go with her fries. And Todd is going back for his third piece of cheesecake, while Liz picks at her salad, no dressing. Josh is having a plate of garbanzo beans because Friday is his legume day. You won't find Anita in the cafeteria because she never eats lunch. She has a candy bar at break, which tides her over until 4:00, and then she gets a burger on the way home.

Are you starving yourself spiritually?

Look It Up: You can't find too many examples in the Bible of people worrying about getting enough complex carbohydrates, or despairing over stubborn cellulite. Since most people walked everywhere they went, they got plenty of exercise. They didn't need special diets because they used common sense:

• "For everything God created is good, and nothing is to be rejected if it is received with thanksgiving" (1 Timothy 4:4). Not everything that man creates is good, such as over-processed food, or diet food substitutes.

• "When you sit to dine with a ruler, note well what is before you, and put a knife to your throat if you are given to gluttony" (Proverbs 23: 1-2).

Think It Through: God wants us to enjoy the best health we can. For most teens, that means getting plenty of good food and exercise. Nutrition is really important in your teen years because you're still growing. Lousy eating habits lead to fatigue, inability to concentrate, and other complications.

Our point is not to give a lecture on nutrition. We just want to say that healthy eating was always smart, long before it became fashionable. Read about Daniel's experience at the king's court (see *Nail it Down*). It just makes sense to take care of yourself!

Work It Out: Take inventory of your present eating and exercise habits. Throw out: yo-yo dieting, sitting around watching T.V., binge eating, meal skipping, and fad dieting. Regular exercise will do amazing things for your self-image, even if you don't lose any weight.

Nail It Down: On Saturday read Daniel 1:3-16. On Sunday read Proverbs 23:20-21.

FIVE FOOD

THE FIRST (& PROBABLY LAST)

WORDY AWARDS

Most Cameo Appearances

Presented to King David for being
mentioned 1,118 times in the Bible

Forget Oscars, Emmys, Grammys, Golden Globes, and Tonys! It's time for the "Wordys"—those outrageous awards for the wide world of Scripture.

The "Most Cameo Appearances" Award—to King David, for being mentioned 1,118 times in the Bible.

The "It's Time to Do a Few Sit-ups" Award—to King Eglon, who was at least 200 pounds overweight (Judges 3:17).

The "You People Are Disgusting!" Award—to the cannibalistic women in 2 Kings 6:26-30.

The "I Wouldn't Want to be in Your Shoes" Award—to poor Job, a victim of a Satanic attack, a nagging wife, and insensitive friends.

The "Aw, I'm Nothing Special" Award—to Moses, the most humble man in the world (Numbers 12:3). Don't tell him . . . he might start getting a big head!

The "Hey, These Special Effects Are Just a Little Too Scary!" Award —to Belshazzar, who had a bad case of knocking knees in Daniel 5–6.

The "What a Great Line" Award — to Psalm 110:1, which is quoted 18 times in the rest of the Bible.

The "Boy, That Was Quick!" Award—to the book of Third John (only 299 words).

The "Most Popular Script" Award—to Isaiah, referred to over 415 times in the New Testament.

The "Are You Sure You're Not Related to Einstein?" Award—to the woman at the well in Sychar for responding, "I can see that you are a prophet" after Jesus met her and accurately described her loose lifestyle within two minutes (see John 4:1-29).

A MEDITATION
FOR YOUR SITUATION

Here's where to look in the Bible if you're:

• Struggling with recurring sin —Romans 6:1-14.

• Wondering if God really loves you—Romans 8:31-39.

• Having trouble trusting God —Psalm 37.

• Trying to understand what faith is—Hebrews 11.

• Not getting along with others —Colossians 3:12-17.

• Questioning what heaven is like—Revelation 21–22.

• In need of forgiveness— Psalms 32 and 51.

• Feeling weak or tired—Isaiah 40:29-31.

• Asking, "Why do the wicked prosper?"—Psalm 73.

• Forgetting how precious you are to God—Ephesians 1:3-14.

• Looking for motivation to live for Christ—2 Corinthians 5:11-21.

• Wrestling with peer pressure— Romans 12.

• Afraid—Isaiah 41:10.

GOD

You Can Know Him

"Grace and peace be yours in abundance through the knowledge of God and of Jesus our Lord" (2 Peter 1:2).

The most important concept humans must wrestle with is God: Who is He? What is He like? How can we know Him?

And yet if we finite creatures attempt to fully understand the infinite Creator, we find ourselves with mental meltdown. For what we are trying to do is comprehend the incomprehensible.

Fortunately, God has not left us to struggle in ignorance. He has revealed much about His nature in the pages of the Bible. Would you like to see what He says about Himself?

On a camping trip to the mountains, Kyle gets up early one morning and hikes up to Eagle's Peak. From there he has a panoramic view of the hills and valleys to the east.

As a cool morning breeze blows gently through his hair, Kyle sits back against a boulder to watch the sun rise. This spectacular display is made all the more dramatic by an unearthly silence that blankets the ridge.

Just before seven, a large trout begins splashing about in the mountain pool nearby. As he stares at the beauty on every side, Kyle begins to wonder about God.

Our awesome Creator

Look It Up: It's not surprising that such a place as Eagle's Peak prompts Kyle to consider God. The beauties of nature are supposed to have that effect:

- "The heavens declare the glory of God; the skies proclaim the work of his hands" (Psalm 19:1).
- "You alone are the LORD. You made the heavens, even the highest heavens, and all their starry host, the earth and all that is on it, the seas and all that is in them. You give life to everything, and the multitudes of heaven worship you" (Nehemiah 9:6).

Think It Through: The Bible indicates that the wonders of creation are designed to make us reflect on our Creator. Isn't it strange that while all nature is shouting out the glory and power of God, most scientists are trusting in the theory of evolution, and New Age devotees are worshiping the universe?

When was the last time you acknowledged God for who He is—the mighty Creator of the universe? Think of some places you like to visit: the beach, the mountains, the lake. God designed and made them for us to enjoy. They belong to Him.

Work It Out: This week we want to gain a better understanding of who God is and how we relate to Him.

Just for today, try to forget about about clothes, cars, high-rise buildings, television, and Nintendo. Spend some time contemplating God's magnificent creation—the sky, the clouds, the birds, and flowers. Then pray this prayer:

"God, I praise You as the mighty Creator of the universe. Your power is limitless, and Your creativity is staggering. Thank You for revealing Yourself through nature. Help me to know You better. Amen."

Nail It Down: Read Romans 1:20.

✝ ✝ ✝ ✝ ✝ ONE GOD ✝ ✝ ✝ ✝ ✝ ✝ ✝ ✝ ✝ ✝ ✝ ✝

L et's look inside some of the homes on Oakwood Drive:

• Clara's dad is abusive. He yells a lot, and when he really gets angry, he strikes whomever is within reach.

• Because his parents are divorced, David sees his dad only on holidays. On these occasions his dad seems distant and cold. It hurts David to feel that his father doesn't care.

• Amy's father is full of praise when she makes good grades or gets any kind of award, but if she slips up, he becomes stingingly critical. His attitude seems to say, "You're a total loser. Get lost!"

Our perfect Father

Look It Up: Even though our earthly dads can sometimes let us down, we Christians have a perfect Father in God:

• "Yet, O LORD, you are our Father" (Isaiah 64:8).

• "Yet for us there is but one God, the Father, from whom all things came and for whom we live" (1 Corinthians 8:6).

• "There is . . . one God and Father of all, who is over all and through all and in all" (Ephesians 4:4, 6).

Think It Through: God's ideal plan is that our earthly fathers become a reflection of His own Fatherhood. Unfortunately humans, being imperfect, can't always be perfect fathers. Since God has placed you in your father's care, He expects you to respect and obey your father even when you feel he is being unfair.

Many Christians believe that the way you relate to your earthly father affects how you view God. If your father is absent, strict, mean, unfair, or quick-tempered, pehaps you think of God as having those traits. But He doesn't. He is always with us, always kind and loving, always completely patient and fair.

Work It Out: Some of the fathers portrayed on TV almost never make serious mistakes—Dr. Huxtable, Doogie Howser's father, and Mike Seaver's dad. But realize this: Only your heavenly Father is perfect.

Have a time of prayer with your heavenly Father. Thank Him for giving you a father to care and provide for you. If you don't know your father, or if he has died, ask God to help you accept Him as your Father. Thank God for being your perfect, loving, eternal Father.

Nail It Down: Read Romans 8:14-16.

Pray About It:

✝ ✝ ✝ ✝ ✝ T W O

While studying for his ancient history final, Conrad dozed off. Within minutes he was dreaming. There he stood among the throng that lined the Appian way. It was 48 B.C. and Caesar was returning from his victory over Pompey at Pharsalia.

As the Emperor's chariot neared, the huge crowd bowed to the ground in unison. Shouts of adulation—"Hail, Caesar!" and "Long live Caesar!" filled the air as the Emperor rolled toward Rome, resplendent in his golden chariot. Conrad awoke with goose bumps.

Our majestic King

Look It Up: Your history book gives accounts of the kings and queens who reigned over empires both great and small. But to hear about the most glorious King of all, you have to consult the Bible:

"How awesome is the LORD Most High, the great King over all the earth! . . . Sing praises to God, sing praises; sing praises to our King, sing praises. For God is the King of all the earth; sing to him a psalm of praise. God reigns over the nations; God is seated on his holy throne. The nobles of the nations assemble as the people of the God of Abraham, for the kings of the earth belong to God; he is greatly exalted" (Psalm 47:2, 6-9).

Think It Through: There are certain standards of behavior, called *protocol*, that people use when they are introduced to royalty. What do you think the response would be if, upon meeting Queen Elizabeth, Hillary Clinton said, "Hey, Liz, don't you think it's about time you ditched that purse?" And can you imagine any British subject saying to Princess Diana, "Why don't you just get it yourself?"

If we honor our earthly rulers with the appropriate respect and courtesy, how much more should we honor and obey God, the ruler of the universe?

Work It Out: Treat God like the great King that He is. Are you ignoring certain divine decrees by not carrying out a command, or doing a forbidden thing? Identify those wrong acts, and begin obeying—today!

When you pray do you speak to God in a flippant, irreverent manner? Begin praying with the realization that you are addressing the majestic King of Kings.

Nail It Down: Read Psalm 145:1-2.

✝ ✝ ✝ ✝ ✝ ✝ THREE **GOD** ✝ ✝ ✝ ✝ ✝ ✝ ✝ ✝ ✝

Pittsville is upset over the verdicts in two local trials.

A week ago, Judge Cornelius P. Bickford sentenced a tenth-grader to a year in reform school for shoplifting a $2 tube of lipstick.

"Young lady, I realize this is your first offense, but all criminal acts will be punished while I am judge."

Yesterday, the judge dropped drunk driving charges against a member of the town council.

"Mr. Campbell, your problem requires professional treatment. I encourage you to seek such help."

Our righteous Judge

Look It Up: Unfair decisions by human judges should only serve to remind us of our impartial divine Judge—the Lord God, who will one day right every wrong.

• "God is a righteous judge, a God who expresses his wrath [on violence and wickedness] every day" (Psalm 7:11).

• "Then men will say, 'Surely the righteous still are rewarded; surely there is a God who judges the earth'" (Psalm 58:11).

• "They will sing before the LORD, for he comes, he comes to judge the earth. He will judge the world in righteousness and the peoples in his truth" (Psalm 96:13).

Think It Through: Justice is a major theme in the Bible. God's people are required to deal fairly with others. Injustice is always denounced.

What about you? Do you ever take advantage of people for your own selfish gain? Remember: we must be fair. One day we will stand before Christ and be judged on our behavior as believers (2 Corinthians 5:10).

Work It Out: The fact that our God is a righteous Judge should affect your life today. You should:

• Gently and humbly state your objection to unfair policies and practices—at school, in government, at church, and in your community. (Don't criticize until you have earnestly prayed with mature believers about the situations you feel are unjust.)

• Trust God to bring about justice in His timing.

• Exercise fairness in your own relationships, especially with younger brothers and sisters.

• Praise God that no wrong acts escape His notice.

Nail It Down: Read Psalm 94:2.

Pray About It:

✝ ✝ ✝ ✝ ✝ FOUR

Bill: "Let's say you have a major problem. Who are you going to talk to first?"

Beth: "Either Christy or Julie, I guess. They're probably my best friends. But it makes me so mad because sometimes Christy can't keep a secret. And Julie's so busy with her new boyfriend, I hardly see her anymore."

Bill: "What about God?"

Beth: "Well, sure, I'd pray and everything. But God is . . . not really a *friend*. I don't think of Him like I do Christy and Julie."

Our faithful Friend

Look It Up: When we focus on God's roles as Creator, Father, King, and Judge, it's easy to forget that He can also be a Friend.

1. Abraham enjoyed a friendship with God: "And the scripture was fulfilled that says, 'Abraham believed God, and it was credited to him as righteousness,' and he was called God's friend" (James 2:23).

2. Moses enjoyed a friendship with God: "The LORD would speak to Moses face to face, as a man speaks with his friend" (Exodus 33:11).

3. Jesus Christ emphasized friendship between God and His people: "I no longer call you servants. . . . Instead, I have called you friends" (John 15:15).

Think It Through: What an amazing truth: We can actually be friends with the God of the universe! (Anyone who can't get excited about that needs to think again.)

What are the things that make a friendship close? Are those ingredients a part of your relationship with God? If not, why?

Work It Out: Good friends spend time together and talk to each other, right? So do those things with God today and every day:

• Get your Bible and go to a quiet place. Tell God what you're thinking. Then ask Him to reveal what's on His mind by guiding your reading of the Scriptures.

• But don't stop there. Converse with Him all day—as you drive, as you walk to classes, while opening your locker, just like you do with your other friends. Because that's what He is: our most faithful Friend.

Nail It Down: For more insight into God's nature read Psalm 103 on Saturday and Isaiah 40 on Sunday.

✝ ✝ ✝ ✝ ✝ ✝ FIVE **GOD** ✝ ✝ ✝ ✝ ✝ ✝ ✝ ✝ ✝ ✝

THE BIBLE
Not Just Any Book

Everyone has an opinion about the Bible:

- "It's the longest book I've ever seen."
- "Nobody reads our family Bible. It's on a shelf all covered with dust. It weighs about 50 pounds."
- "It's all about God and the miracles He's done."
- "It's full of contradictions. Plus, it's too hard to understand."
- "It's just a bunch of myths and fairy tales."

In this topic, we'll try to answer some of the most common questions people have about the Bible. Maybe they're your questions too.

"The grass withers and the flowers fall, but the word of our God stands forever" (Isaiah 40:8).

I don't under-
stand your
church," John
explains to
Michael. "Every-
thing is the Bible
this and the Bible
that. Don't get me
wrong. I think it's
good to read
the Bible some-
times. But there
are other helpful
books too.

"Take our minis-
ter, for example.
Most of the time he
doesn't even refer
to the Bible in his
sermons. He uses
modern stories to
inspire us to live
good lives.

"I guess that's
the big difference
between my church
and your church.
You guys act like
the Bible is the
greatest book in the
world."

What's so great about the Bible?

Look It Up: Throughout the entire Bible we find statements like these: "This is what the Lord says" or " . . .
the Word was with God and the Word was God." The
Bible is God's means of communication with us. In it
we can see what our invisible God is like. It reveals His
character, discloses His thoughts and plans for planet
Earth, and unravels many of life's mysteries.

To answer John, the Bible *is* the greatest book in the
world. It is the actual Word of God to mankind:

"And we also thank God continually because, when
you received the word of God, which you heard from
us, you accepted it not as the word of men, but as it
actually is, the word of God, which is at work in you
who believe" (1 Thessalonians 2:13).

Think It Through: When we watch a beautiful sunset,
or think about the complexity of the human body, our
thoughts often turn to God. Psalm 19:1-6 agrees that
nature reveals much about His glory, power, and ethi-
cal standards.

But what if that's all we had to go on? What could
we know about God if the only information we had
about Him was what we see in nature?

He has graciously given us a special revelation of
Himself—the written Scriptures. Through the Bible we
gain a clearer, more complete picture of our Creator.

Work It Out: Make this your prayer:

"Lord, help me gain a better understanding and a
deeper appreciation for Your Word this week. I realize
that the Bible is not just another book. It is Your revelation to mankind. I recommit myself right now to learning what You have to say to me about my life. Amen."

Nail It Down: Compare Hebrews 1:1-2 with John 1:1-2.

□ □ □ □ □ □ ONE **THE BIBLE** □ □ □ □ □

As soon as Michael stated that the Bible is God's Word to the world, John launched into this argument:

"Now wait a minute. One minute you talk about the Bible as the Word of God. Then in the very next breath you refer to the psalms of King David, the Apostle Paul's letters, the Gospel of John. Those sound like human authors to me. Sorry, but you can't have it both ways. Either the Bible is the Word of God, or it's the writings and opinions of a bunch of men."

Who really wrote the Bible?

Look It Up: John's argument sounds logical. The Bible must be either a human or a divine document, right? Not necessarily. It's both human and divine. Consider this:

"All Scripture is God-breathed and is useful for teaching, rebuking, correcting and training in right-eousness" (2 Timothy 3:16).

God-breathed means that God is the ultimate author of the Bible. He employed diverse human authors to do the actual writing. But He provided the inspiration, breathing out His word through human channels.

Think It Through: This idea of inspiration, of God "breathing out" the Scriptures, does not mean that He dictated and men merely copied. The human authors crafted the Word of God using their own styles of writing. During this process, they were under the constant supervision and direction of the Holy Spirit.

The fact that the Bible is inspired by God is what makes it the greatest, most important book in existence.

Work It Out: Have you read the entire Bible cover to cover? If not, make that commitment right now. Think about it: In just 12 months, you can discover God's written message to the world:

• Find a friend who will take this step with you.

• Get a paperback Bible designed to be read in one year. (You can find one at most Christian bookstores.)

• Pray. Ask God to give you the guidance and understanding you need to approach His Word. He greatly desires to speak to you through the Bible.

Nail It Down: Read 2 Peter 1:21.

Pray About It: ——————————————

TWO

❑ ❑ ❑ ❑ ❑

When Michael insisted that the Bible is the inspired Word of God, John countered with this:

"Look, everybody knows the Bible is full of errors and contradictions. Say whatever you want about it being 'breathed out' by God, the fact is the men who wrote it made a lot of mistakes—historically and scientifically. We just can't trust it completely."

Do we know the Bible is really true?

Look It Up: Actually, John, we *can* trust the Bible as 100 percent accurate and reliable. Consider this one verse:

"[I am the LORD] . . . who says of Cyrus, 'He is my shepherd and will accomplish all that I please; he will say of Jerusalem, "Let it be rebuilt," and of the temple, "Let its foundations be laid" ' " (Isaiah 44:28).

This prophecy was given in 700 B.C. About 100 years later Jerusalem was destroyed by the Babylonians. Some sixty years after that, King Cyrus of Persia decreed the rebuilding of Jerusalem—including the temple. A coincidence? Not when you consider that the Bible contains literally hundreds of fulfilled prophecies.

Think It Through: Archaeologists have further authenticated the Biblical record. Here is another example:

At one time critics rejected the reliability of Luke's Gospel, charging that Quirinius was not governor of Syria at the time of Jesus' birth (Luke 2:1-3). However, an inscription uncovered during an archaeological dig in Antioch has proved Luke's account.

Work It Out: Many skeptics try to discredit the reliability of the Bible without really investigating the facts. Such criticism causes some Christians to doubt their faith. Get informed so that you have an answer to such charges.

The book *Answers to Tough Questions Skeptics Ask about the Christian Faith,* by Josh McDowell and Don Stewart, discusses many of the so-called contradictions and errors in the Bible. Examine the evidence for yourself and decide whether the Bible really does contain "mistakes." Pick up this faith-builder and read it this month.

Nail It Down: Compare Micah 5:2 with Matthew 2:1.

□ □ □ □ □ □ THREE **THE BIBLE** □ □ □ □ □

Hi, I'm Michael.

"I think it's about time I step in here and show you exactly what I mean. Enough theory about Bible study—let's actually do some! How about starting with this verse:

'Do not let this Book of the Law depart from your mouth; meditate on it day and night, so that you may be careful to do everything written in it. Then you will be prosperous and successful'
(Joshua 1:8)."

Three steps for Bible study

STEP ONE: Observation—What Does It Say?
• Read the passage/verse at least two times.
• Write down all the facts and details you observe. This means you answer questions like: "Who is talking? When is this taking place? What is being said?"

STEP TWO: Interpretation—What Does It Mean?
Most of the time, the meaning of a passage is easy to see. However, these basic rules help when you read:
• Make sure you know Christ and have His Spirit as your Teacher (1 Corinthians 2:14).
• Let obvious verses help explain obscure ones.
• Make sure you base your experience on the Bible; don't use personal experience to interpret the Bible.
• Don't look for hidden, symbolic meanings when the passage is straightforward.
• Rely on the immediate context of a verse or passage when you need help to determine its meaning.
• Use dictionaries, other translations, commentaries, and Bible concordances to further enhance your study.
Now take five minutes to think about what Joshua 1:8 means.

STEP THREE: Application—What Must I Do?
When you have correctly observed and interpreted the verse, you must determine:
• Is there a command here to obey?
• Is there a sin to avoid?
• Is there a promise to claim?
• Is there an example to follow?
• What must I do in relation to this verse to make its truth a part of my life (James 1:22-25)?
Finally, take two minutes, reflect on Joshua 1:8, and figure out what you need to do.
Congratulations! You are a bona fide Bible student.

Pray About It:

FOUR

❏ ❏ ❏ ❏ ❏

M ichael is a good example of the difference the Bible can make in a person's life.

Two years ago, he was your basic shallow Christian. He went to church and avoided smoking, drinking, drugs, and sex. But that negative description pretty much summed up his faith.

Now that Michael is getting into the Word on a regular basis, everyone can see positive things happening in his life. Most exciting of all, he's becoming more and more like Christ. The transformation is slow but steady, and certainly noticeable.

Does the Bible make a difference?

Look It Up: Here are just some of the changes the Word has worked in Michael's life:

• Memorizing Scripture has helped him overcome certain temptations. "I have hidden your word in my heart that I might not sin against you" (Psalm 119:11).

• Reading the Bible has caused Michael to grow deeper in his faith (1 Peter 2:2).

• Meditating on God's Word has given Michael direction when he's been faced with big decisions (Psalm 119:105).

• Studying the Bible has equipped Michael to minister to others (2 Timothy 3:17).

Think It Through: When all else has faded into oblivion—cars, clothes, parties, schoolwork, money, popularity—God's Word will remain (Matthew 24:35). Does the Bible have its rightful place on your list of priorities?

Why do you think so many Christians in this culture are indifferent about the Bible? What makes believers in oppressed countries willing to risk almost anything to get even a few pages of Scripture?

Work It Out: The Bible can truly change your life! Give the Scriptures a chance to work in you.

1. Go back and quickly review the lessons about the Bible in the previous four pages. What truth stands out to you the most?

2. Find a Christian friend and explain why that truth means so much to you today.

3. Set aside fifteen minutes today and read Psalm 119. It's all about the wonderful Word of God.

Nail It Down: This weekend, spend some extra time with God and His Word. Read Hebrews 4:12 on Saturday and James 1:22-25 on Sunday.

⊐ ❑ ❑ ❑ ❑ ❑ FIVE **THE BIBLE** ❑ ❑ ❑ ❑ ❑

YOU'RE HOT STUFF

The night was crisp and crystal clear. I was driving to Los Angeles from Palm Springs about 11:00 P.M. The temperature was cool.

About 20 miles outside of Palm Springs, the city lights were gone and there wasn't another car in sight. It was just me, the hum of my Toyota, and the passion and power of Beethoven's *Symphony No. 1*.

Then I noticed the sky. The night canopy was filled with a million stars, all shining points of beautiful light. I gasped and began slowing down. I had to get out and take a look.

Having pulled off a safe distance from the highway, I turned the car off and got out. Then I looked around to make sure nobody was watching. Comfortably sure I was alone, I got on my knees, raised my hands, and sang as loud as I could: "Praise God from whom all blessings flow! . . ."

You are more glorious than nature. Most people don't react to nature's glory by shouting the Doxology. But all of us have been awestruck at a star-filled sky, a smoky gorge or valley, a rainbow-colored sunset, a glimpse of the Northern Lights.

Yes, nature is glorious. But did you know that you are much more glorious than the most awesome natural event?

What makes something significant? About the expanse of the universe, the Bible says, *"God set [the sun, moon, and stars] in the expanse of the sky to give light to the earth"* (Genesis 1:16-17). From God's perspective, then, the earth is more significant than the stars, even though the earth is smaller. Likewise, people are more significant than the earth, even though they are smaller. *"Let us make man in our image, in our likeness, and let them rule over . . . all the earth"* (v. 26).

You're hot stuff! Do you see what that means? You, a single person, are more valuable than the whole expanse of the universe. Being made in God's own image, you have (1) a more valuable essence; and (2) a more important calling than the rest of God's creation.

The bottom line. Nature is God's; therefore, it must be treated with respect. Man rules nature; therefore, animals and the rest of the environment exist for us to use, enjoy, and develop. Our view of ourselves, the animal kingdom, and the rest of the environment should take these truths into account.

Hey! I guess that means that the next time I see you, I should extend my arms toward you and sing, "Praise God from whom all blessings flow! . . ."

That's this editor's viewpoint. Maybe you could see it that way too.

BIBLE TRIVIA

1. What kind of lights did Noah use on the ark?

1. Flood lights.

2. Who had surgery performed on him while he slept?

2. Adam (Genesis 2:21)

3. Which king had the first birthday party in the Bible?

3. Pharaoh, at the time Joseph was in Egypt (Genesis 40:20)

4. Which Old Testament woman bore a child at age 90 and is mentioned more than any other woman in the Bible (56 times)?

4. Sarah

5. Who is the only man mentioned in the Bible as being naturally bald?

5. Elisha (2 Kings 2:23)

6. Which American president published an edition of the Gospels that left out all the supernatural elements?

6. Thomas Jefferson

7. What was the "Unrighteous Bible"?

7. An edition, printed at Cambridge in 1653, containing the printer's error, "*Know ye not that the unrighteous shall inherit the kingdom of God?*" (*1 Corinthians 6:9*)

8. In the immensely popular *The Greatest Story Ever Told* (1965), practically every star in Hollywood had a small role. What role, with only one line of dialogue, did John Wayne play in this movie about Jesus?

8. The centurion at Jesus' crucifixion (who said, "Truly, this was the Son of God.")

The above questions have been excerpted from J. Stephen Lang's The Complete Book of Bible Trivia. *Used by permission of Tyndale House Publishers, Inc. All rights reserved.*

NEW AGE
Exposing an Ancient Error

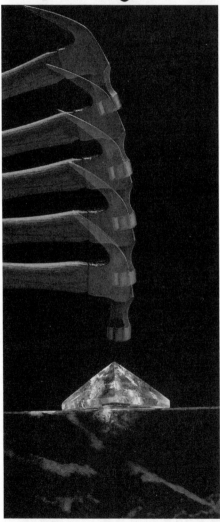

What does it mean when:

• Your aunt reads Shirley MacLaine's best-seller, *Dancing in the Light?*

• The clerk at the health food store gives you a flyer advertising an upcoming human potential conference?

• Your new doctor keeps talking about "hypnotherapy"?

Any one of these experiences means that you've just had an encounter with New Age thought. It also means that the next few pages may be the most informative reading you've done in a long time.

"But I am afraid that just as Eve was deceived by the serpent's cunning, your minds may somehow be led astray from your sincere and pure devotion to Christ" (2 Corinthians 11:3).

The Chapmans are church members though they really don't go very often. Mr. Chapman is trying to get his new business off the ground. The kids are busy with swim team, studies, and jobs. And Mrs. Chapman is into something really strange.

Lately she's been reading books on reincarnation and hanging crystals everywhere. But that's nothing compared to what happened last Thursday afternoon.

Marilyn, 15, got home early. When she walked in the living room, her mom was staring out the window chanting, "I am god. I am god."

New light or old darkness?

Look It Up: Based on Hindu philosophy, New Age thought is winning millions of converts by denying death and proclaiming that "we are all god."

In truth, this "new" message is an old lie. It's precisely the tactic that the Devil used in the Garden of Eden. When Eve told the serpent that disobeying God would result in death, he responded:

" 'You will not surely die,' the serpent said to the woman. 'For God knows that when you eat of it your eyes will be opened, and you will be like God, knowing good and evil' " (Genesis 3:4-5).

Think It Through: It's not surprising that a lost world would much rather hear the New Age message than the gospel. Here's why: New Age thought says, "You are magnificent. You are god." The Bible says, "You are sinful. You need God." Big difference. New Age sounds so much more positive, while Christianity seems offensive (2 Corinthians 2:16) to unbelievers.

But the issue really isn't which sounds better or which idea makes people feel better about themselves. The issue is which is true.

Work It Out: Before we go any further in our investigation of the New Age movement, we need to pray. Express these feelings to God:

"Lord, help me to understand this week the critical difference between the truth in Your Word and the deceptiveness of Eastern thought. Give me some solid ammunition so that I can fight back when people start talking about astrology, meditation, channeling, and all other New Age practices. Guard my mind and remind me again and again that You are the Truth. Amen."

Nail It Down: Read 1 Corinthians 1:23.

✦ ✦ ✦ ✦ ✦ ✦ **ONE NEW AGE** ✦ ✦ ✦ ✦

Rob spends Friday night watching videos on cable. First up is *The Dark Crystal*. At the end, the kindly Mystics and the diabolical Murgazoids are fused into one group. Rob doesn't realize it, but he's just been taught a New Age precept called *monism*—the idea that everything (including good and evil) is one.

During *The Empire Strikes Back*, Rob learns about *pantheism*—the idea that the Force is all and all is god. Says Yoda, "Its energy surrounds us and binds us. Luminous beings we are, not this crude matter. Feel it you must. Feel the flow."

The battle of the "-isms"

Look It Up: According to the Bible, both monism and pantheism are false. In other words, the Force is a farce.

• Rejecting monism, Genesis states that our universe is not an undivided unity, but a diverse creation of separate, distinct creatures and things (Genesis 1:1-31).

• Condemning pantheism, Ecclesiastes asserts that God and His creation are not the same: "God is in heaven and you are on earth" (Ecclesiastes 5:2).

Think It Through: The Bible supports *theism*, the concept that (read this slowly) God is a personal, moral, knowable Creator who possesses unlimited power, intelligence, and (something else that the New Age movement avoids talking about)—love.

This true God of the Bible is nothing like the New Age concept of an inert, impersonal energy or force that encompasses both good and evil.

Which "-ism" do you believe in?

Work It Out: Christians need to be aware that New Age philosophy is dangerous and abhorrent to God.

• Be on the lookout for New Age concepts in films, television, and public school classrooms.

•If you hear something that sounds strange, talk it over with your parents and/or youth leader.

•Don't accept "new" statements or ideas without carefully examining them and comparing them to the standard of God's Word.

•Remember: Many times this mystical philosophy is presented so that it masquerades as something harmless. Don't be deceived.

Nail It Down: Read Romans 1:25.

Pray About It:

❖ ❖ ❖ ❖ T W O

While researching Eastern thought for a report in his religion class, Doug is astounded to come across these statements in various New Age literature:

• "Kneel to your own self. Honor and worship your own being. God dwells within you as you" (Swami Muktananda).

• "Each person is a universe. If you know yourself, you know everything" (Shirley MacLaine).

• "We are gods and might as well get good at it" (The Next Whole Earth Catalogue).

• "We are like a god, omnipotent and omniscient" (George Leonard).

A mixed-up view of mankind

Look It Up: The Bible's view of humanity is radically different from the New Age view:

• We are not God. We are the finite, beloved creatures of an infinite, loving God (Genesis 1:26-28; Isaiah 2:22; John 3:16).

• Our great need is not looking inward and realizing that we are God, but looking upward and realizing we need God (Luke 18:9-14).

• We are not reincarnated through death to face endless lives. We will be resurrected after death to face the judgment of God. "Man is destined to die once, and after that to face judgment" (Hebrews 9:27).

Think It Through: Crystals, channeling, astral projection, transcendental meditation, yoga, past-life regression, rebirthing, EST, Silva mind control, hypnosis, bioenergetics—these are some of the techniques employed by New Age advocates in their attempts to achieve God-realization or "enlightenment."

Do you know people involved in these activities? Are you?

Work It Out: Go to a Christian bookstore and purchase the inexpensive booklet entitled *The New Age Movement*, by Douglas R. Groothuis. This helpful publication summarizes the basic features of Eastern mysticism, Western style.

Or, if you wish to explore the movement in detail, try these books by the same author, *Unmasking the New Age* and *Confronting the New Age*. Form a study group with other believers and become more informed about this flourishing philosophy.

Nail It Down: Check out God's reponse when Herod allowed people to call him a god—Acts 12:21-23.

❖ ❖ ❖ ❖ ❖ ❖ THREE **NEW AGE** ❖ ❖ ❖

When Marie went to the doctor because of fatigue, she thought he'd prescribe vitamins and exercise. Instead, he recommended yoga and something called "visualization therapy."

• Jim picked up a brochure that called for "global political transformation." The tract advocated a one-world government as the only solution to mankind's problems.

• Stephanie's dad, a salesman for a major corporation, left today for a company-sponsored seminar on "The Philosophy of Unlimited Human Potential."

The New Age "tidal wave"

Look It Up: Medicine, politics, education, business, religion, science, economics, entertainment—name a sector of society and New Age thought has infiltrated it. This Eastern invasion means that you need to be extremely careful whom and what you listen to:

"Dear friends, do not believe every spirit, but test the spirits to see whether they are from God, because many false prophets have gone out into the world" (1 John 4:1).

A similar warning is found in 2 Timothy 4:3-4.

Think It Through: Did you know that all over the country, numerous New Age churches are springing up? And through certain visualization exercises, New Age thought has even invaded some Christian youth groups.

Are you aware that through books like Fritjof Capra's *The Tao of Physics* and Michael Talbot's *Mysticism and the New Physics*, many in the scientific community are accepting New Age thought?

In short, Eastern mysticism is everywhere. You can run, but you can't hide!

Work It Out: Books and videos about the New Age movement are excellent topics of discussion at home, school, and in youth groups. Ask your parents or youth leader to rent the video entitled *Gods of the New Age*. This fascinating documentary, available at most Christian bookstores, will help you understand more about the roots, practices, and dangers of Eastern thought.

Arrange with your friends to keep each other up to date on the latest New Age developments.

Nail It Down: Read 2 John 9-11.

Pray About It:

❖ ❖ ❖ ❖

F O U R

"I'm starving," Celia announces. "Want to get a pizza?"

Kimberly responds nervously. "Uh, no. I can't. I've got to catch a bus . . . to my class at the health club."

"When did you start doing aerobics? You know, I ought to go with you," Celia says looking at her thighs. "I need exercise a whole lot more than I need pizza."

"Um, well, it's not really aerobics. It's a class in yoga. You know—learning how to relax and breathe and stuff like that."

A bus ticket to destruction

Look It Up: Kimberly needs to be careful about Yoga. Teachings that involve emptying the mind in order to achieve peace with the universe are false and destructive.

Let's make two final observations about the New Age movement:

1. God has already foreseen that such false teaching would be incredibly popular. (1 Timothy 4:1-2).

2. The end result for those who embrace bogus philosophies is destruction: "They [false teachers] will secretly introduce destructive heresies, even denying the sovereign Lord who bought them—bringing swift destruction on themselves. . . . Their condemnation has long been hanging over them" (2 Peter 2:1, 3).

Think It Through: "Lend me $100 to invest and in two weeks I'll bring you $200." The guy seems honest. It sounds like a good deal. Sure enough, he doubles your money. Next time he asks for $500. You give it to him and, amazingly, he brings you back $1000! When he asks for $5000, you can't give it to him fast enough . . . but you never see the man or your cash again.

That's what happens when people get involved in New Age practices. Slowly, Satan gains their trust. Then, when they drop their guard, he wipes them out.

Work It Out: If you know people who are playing with some form of Eastern mysticism, do these things:
• Pray that God will lead them out of a dangerous situation.
• Talk with them and encourage them to abandon the deceitful practices of the New Age movement. Give them some of the materials described this week to warn them of the jeopardy they're in.

Nail It Down: Read 2 Peter 3:17-18 and 2 Timothy 3:1-9.

❖ ❖ ❖ ❖ ❖ ❖ FIVE **NEW AGE** ❖ ❖ ❖ ❖

SOCIETY
Is Time Running Out?

We're going to give it to you straight. No beating around the bush, no candy-coating the truth.

Our nation is heading down the pipes. We've hit the skids. We're in big trouble.

The bottom line is that we've told God to take a hike. "Thanks, Lord, but we really don't need You. We can handle things on our own."

Yeah, right. We've handled things all right . . . we've basically turned our society into a cesspool. Kind of makes you wonder how much longer God is going to let things go on.

Are our days numbered?

"Righteousness exalts a nation, but sin is a disgrace to any people" (Proverbs 14:34).

Sandra woke up feeling pretty good. By the time she got to school, however, she was in a rotten mood. What happened?

Perhaps it has something to do with the fact that she watched *Have a Nice Day, USA* on T.V. at breakfast and saw: a story about a mother who sued her doctor because her baby survived an abortion; the latest statistics on the spread of AIDS; a report on two drug-related shootings; reports on an overnight kidnaping, gang rape, and murder; and a feature story on the victims of incest.

And that was just in the first half hour.

You call this a Christian nation?

Look It Up: Perhaps you can relate to Sandra's feelings of frustration and despair. So could the psalmist:

"Help, LORD, for the godly are no more; the faithful have vanished from among men" (Psalm 12:1).

Maybe you think it's time for things to change. So did the psalmist:

"It is time for you to act, O LORD; your law is being broken. . . . Streams of tears flow from my eyes, for your law is not obeyed" (Psalm 119:126, 136).

Think It Through: Recent polls tell us that a large number of people in this country claim to be born-again believers in Jesus Christ. If that's true, how come our culture is morally bankrupt?

Some theologians, scientists, and humanitarians continue to insist that mankind is basically good, that we can solve our own problems, and that things are slowly but surely improving with the passage of time. Do you think that's an accurate assessment of our society? Or do you wonder if these individuals live on the same planet that you live on?

Work It Out: Get the daily paper or your favorite news-magazine and pray through it. How do you do that?

• As you read each story, pray for the individuals involved.

• Ask God to intervene and to restore His justice, peace, and righteousness in that specific situation.

• Remember, we can (and should) work to bring about revival in our society. But until God begins working in individual hearts, there will be no lasting change.

Nail It Down: Does the description of Judah in Isaiah 59:7-15 fit our culture?

ONE SOCIETY

You want us to do what?"

Warren is asking his youth group to do a strange thing. After continual reports of political corruption, Warren has assigned each teenager a different book of the Bible.

"Okay, here's the assignment. Read through the book I gave you and list every verse that makes reference to what God expects of governments, kings, or political leaders. When we get all the references, we're going to type them up, and mail them to our elected officials."

"Hey, that's a pretty cool idea!" someone suggests.

"Where are the godly leaders?"

Look It Up: It *is* a cool idea. Leaders need to be encouraged to do what is right:

"If a king judges the poor with fairness, his throne will always be secure" (Proverbs 29:14).

They also need to be admonished when wrong:

"Your rulers are rebels, companions of thieves; they all love bribes and chase after gifts. They do not defend the cause of the fatherless; the widow's case does not come before them" (Isaiah 1:23).

Think It Through: In Israel's history, the kings set the spiritual tone for the nation. When a ruler obeyed God, the nation generally followed and found prosperity. When a leader turned from God, the people usually did likewise, and faced judgment. Do you think this connection between godly leadership and the blessing of God holds true for all nations (even in today's society)?

Do you think the public has a right to know about the personal character and private lives of politicians? Do the moral standards of a politician affect his or her ability to make good decisions? Why or why not?

Work It Out: Get together with some Christian friends and do what Warren's youth group did. Just think— God might use you to speak to the heart of a powerful politician . . . thereby influencing an entire nation.

Begin the practice of praying for your elected officials on a regular basis (1 Timothy 2:1-4).

Ask God if He might be leading you into politics. It's possible that He might want you to shine for Him there.

Nail It Down: Read more about the kinds of leaders that provoke (Isaiah 10:1-3) and that please (Isaiah 33:15-16) the Lord.

Pray About It: _____

T W O

77

A nita is in a debate for speech class and the topic is teen sexuality. Finally she throws down her notes in disgust:

"Why can't you accept that God's standards are the solution to teen pregnancy and sexually transmitted diseases?" she says in frustration. "When will you realize there is no such thing as 'safe sex?'"

You can imagine how the class reacted: "How naive can you be?"

"Yeah, Anita, you can't just impose your values on the rest of us."

"But they're not *my* values," Anita sighs.

Praying for the prophets of God

Look It Up: God always raises up prophetic voices to speak hard words to hard hearts. And almost always the response is negative.

Noah faced scorn when he preached righteousness to his neighbors (2 Peter 2:5).

Jeremiah's sermons encountered rage. He was beaten and thrown into a muddy cistern. This verse is typical of his career: "As soon as Jeremiah finished telling all the people everything the LORD had commanded him to say, the priests, the prophets and all the people seized him and said, 'You must die!' " (Jeremiah 26:8).

Amos felt the sting of rejection (Amos 7:10-13).

As you can see, proclaiming God's truth to people who are comfortable with sin is never a picnic.

Think It Through: What moral issue do you feel strongly about? What would happen if, like Anita, you took a stand in front of your classmates and friends? Which is worse—to speak up and face possible persecution, or to keep silent and let evil continue unchecked?

Work It Out: Pray daily for the ministries that are working to preserve biblical family values, struggling to restore decency to the media, leading the fight against abortion and injustice. For the leaders of these groups ask: for protection from Satan's attacks; for strength to carry on the battle; for boldness in proclaiming the truth; and for success in their endeavors.

Then pick one issue and let your voice be heard. Imagine what would happen if every Christian teenager took a stand against *one* sinful practice in this society.

Nail It Down: Read Amos' answer to his critics— Amos 7:14-17.

THREE **SOCIETY**

The pastor's message is alarming. "Immorality, abortion, pornography, homosexuality, drug use, murder, incest, divorce, alcoholism, materialism, and atheism all point to one certainty: God is going to judge this nation.

"I don't know when it will be. I don't know what form it will take, whether we will have famine, disease, natural disaster, war, or economic collapse. But I think it's safe to assume that, unless we repent very soon, we're going to fall just like all the other great civilizations."

"Can judgment be far off?"

Look It Up: Will God bring judgment on this country?

One passage suggests that national judgment may sometimes be averted on behalf of a small remnant of true believers. "He [the Lord] answered, 'For the sake of ten [righteous people], I will not destroy it [Sodom]' " (Genesis 18:32).

Another indicates that, in some instances, national judgment is inescapable. Only righteous individuals will be spared. " 'Son of man, if a country sins against me by being unfaithful and I stretch out my hand against it to cut off its food supply and send famine upon it and kill its men and their animals, even if these three men—Noah, Daniel and Job—were in it, they could save only themselves by their righteousness, declares the Sovereign LORD' " (Ezekiel 14:13-14).

As to which category this nation might fall under, only God can say.

Think It Through: Someone has stated, "If God doesn't judge this country in all its sin, then He owes an apology to Sodom and Gomorrah!" (See Genesis 18–19).

Considering that throughout history God has always judged evil nations, is it reasonable to expect that we should get some sort of special exemption?

Work It Out: In light of current events you should:
• Spend time praying for a national revival (James 5:16).
• Begin living in a manner that is pleasing to God (Matthew 5:16).
• Ask your non-Christian friends what they think of society's current trends. Share your concerns and your belief in Christ as the country's only hope (1 Peter 3:15).

Nail It Down: Read Isaiah 13:11.

Pray About It: ─────────────

FOUR

After finishing this week's readings on the state of our nation, Shelley is suffering from 3-D disease: Discouragement, Depression, and Deflation.

She laments, "Our country really is going down the tubes. And it sounds like it may be too late to do anything now. Besides, I'm just one person—and I'm only 14. What can I do?"

It's time we said, "Enough!"

Look It Up: Consider these thoughts:
• Your age is not a handicap. "Don't let anyone look down on you because you are young, but set an example for the believers in speech, in life, in love, in faith and in purity" (1 Timothy 4:12).
• The power of God is what matters. When King Saul told David, "You can't fight Goliath . . . you're only a kid!" David responded, "The LORD who delivered me from the paw of the lion and the paw of the bear will deliver me from the hand of this Philistine" (1 Samuel 17:37).
David got the job . . . and he won the battle.

Think It Through: This is no time for thinking—it's time for action. Read on!

Work It Out: Pick a project or two and go for it.
• Join your school newspaper staff and speak out on moral issues from a biblical perspective.
• Work to elect candidates (local, state, and federal) who share your views.
• See if your school library will let you put copies of this devotional guide on the magazine rack.
• When TV stations show trashy movies, write letters to the station manager and to the program's sponsors to voice your disapproval.
• Join a pro-life group in your area.
• Call your elected officials and urge them to stand for morality.
• Encourage local video stores to refuse to rent out pornographic videos.
• Inform your parents and/or pastor if your school textbooks contain anti-religious or immoral material.

Nail It Down: On Saturday, read 2 Timothy 3:1-5. On Sunday, memorize the first part of Genesis 18:14.

FIVE **SOCIETY**

ORIGINS
Where Did It All Begin?

They are, without doubt, two of the most profound questions we can ask:

> *Where did the universe come from?*
> *How did life originate?*

And when we strip away all the facts, data, and opposing theories, there are but two possible answers to each query:

> *1. Incredible luck.*
> *2. Intricate engineering.*

In science class, Eileen is being exposed to the latest theories about the origin of the universe.

"Students, some scientists believe the Big Bang theory—that the cosmos suddenly exploded into existence, by chance, about 15 billion years ago. Others, like Stephen Hawking of Cambridge University, think the universe has always existed.

"Those are the only two rational possibilities."

What was there in the beginning?

Look It Up: Without chemical details, mentions of atomic theory, descriptions of pulsars, or precise dates, the Bible states another option:

"In the beginning God created the heavens and the earth" (Genesis 1:1).

Someone has suggested that the reason for this lack of technical information is that the Bible wasn't written as a science textbook. It's primarily a revelation from God about how we can know Him.

So while it doesn't answer every little question about origins, the Bible does answer the big one. "The universe is not the product of blind chance. And it hasn't always existed. It was specially created by God."

Think It Through: Follow this reasoning:

• **Anything that comes into existence must have a cause.** This is the scientific principle of causality.

• **The universe came into existence.**

The second law of thermodynamics (the fact that the universe is running out of energy and moving toward disorder) and the rapid expansion of the universe suggest it had an initial point of beginning.

Noted scientists Allen Sandage and Robert Jastrow have examined this and other evidence and concluded that the universe must have had a beginning.

• **Therefore, the universe must have a cause.**

Work It Out: Is the debate over origins important to our faith? Most definitely. Can origins be explained simply and in the spaces of five devotional pages? Not a chance.

All the more reason to pray: "Father, at least, give me a good, general grasp of the main issues this week so that I can withstand the attacks on my faith that are sure to come. Amen."

Nail It Down: Read Genesis 1.

▲▲▲▲▲ ONE **ORIGINS** ▲▲▲▲

Eileen wants to believe the Bible is true, but the pro-evolution lectures she's getting in science class are messing with her mind. Plus she's getting hit from two additional sources:

• She subscribes to *National Geographic*, which constantly refers to evolution and the universe, but never mentions God.

• Her boyfriend says the idea of creation is a joke. He says evolution disproves the Bible—and God.

The foolish premise of evolution

Look It Up: Evolution is disturbing, not just from a scientific perspective (see Day 1), but also from a theological point of view. Why is that? Well, in its purest form, the theory of evolution is atheistic. It opposes any belief in a Divine Creator. Note what God's Word says about such a philosophy:

• "In his pride the wicked does not seek him; in all his thoughts there is no room for God" (Psalm 10:4).

• "The fool says in his heart, 'There is no God'" (Psalm 14:1).

• "Since the creation of the world God's invisible qualities . . . have been clearly seen, being understood from what has been made, so that men are without excuse" (Romans 1:20).

The inevitable conclusion is this: Creationism and the Darwinian theory of evolution cannot be reconciled.

Think It Through: How can so many people look at our complex cosmos and conclude that God doesn't exist?

Romans 1:18-20 gives us the answer. This passage describes how people reject God's revelation of Himself in nature. In short, these people "suppress the truth." All the evidence in the world (and there is a vast amount) isn't sufficient to convince them.

Work It Out: Take an hour today to observe the universe around you. Lie down in some quiet place and look up at the clouds, trees, birds, and blue sky. Shut your eyes and listen to the sounds. Absorb the smells.

Finally, end your devotional time thinking about the great mystery of the universe. Praise the Creator for His wisdom and power and ask Him to break through the hard heart of an atheist or agnostic you know.

Nail It Down: Read Genesis 2.

Pray About It: ─────────────────────

▲ ▲ ▲ ▲ T W O

Confused and concerned, Eileen decides to talk to her science teacher. (Mrs. Dubois's intelligence and willingness to listen make her a favorite with the students.)

After Eileen explains her inner struggle to reconcile the theory of evolution and her belief in creation, Mrs. Dubois points to the *Science Digest* on her desk. "Eileen, I know what you're feeling, believe me. I was brought up in a religious home too. But I came to a point where I had to decide, 'Am I going to base my beliefs on a mythical Bible story, or on the findings of modern science?' "

Are there limits to our knowledge?

Look It Up: Many advocates of the theory of evolution dismiss the belief in special creation on the grounds that it contradicts science and human reason. Nothing is farther from the truth. God is a God of reason; He gave us His Word to reveal truth, and to lead us into it:

• " 'I have not spoken in secret, from somewhere in a land of darkness; . . . I, the LORD, speak the truth; I declare what is right' " (Isaiah 45:19).

• "Jesus answered, '. . . for this I came into the world, to testify to the truth. Everyone on the side of truth listens to me' " (John 18:37).

Think It Through: Some critics label creationism a "religious doctrine" and discount it because it is cited in the Bible. But how does that make a thing untrue? If everything in the Bible is automatically suspect, then we are going to have to re-think morality and ethics. The most basic laws of society are found in the Bible: "Do not murder"; "Do not steal."

We do not have to choose between science and the Bible. It is not science that contradicts God's Word, but *scientism*, the belief that all knowledge must be submitted to the methods of science. The reverse is true: we believe that all knowledge, including scientific knowledge, must be submitted to God's revelation in nature and His Word.

Work It Out: Find out if there are any Christians in your community who are experts on the creation/evolution issue. Ask your youth director or Bible study leader to invite them in for a special series on origins.

Practice (with a Christian friend) what you would say if someone called evolution a "fact" (remember, it's still an unproved theory) and creation a "myth."

Nail It Down: Read Job 42:2-3.

▲ ▲ ▲ ▲ ▲ THREE **ORIGINS** ▲ ▲ ▲ ▲

Eileen still has some questions.

"Has evolution been proved? Isn't it still just a theory?"

In her explanation of the evidence supporting evolution, Mrs. Dubois uses words like *alleles, amino acids, homology,* and *paleobiochemistry.* She concludes, "I think the evidence is pretty clear—every species has evolved from a single living cell that came into existence billions of years ago."

"But *how* did it come into existence?" Eileen wants to know.

A horse of a different color

Look It Up: The Bible is not against *micro-evolution*—the idea that certain species undergo change. What the Bible refutes is *macro-evolution*—the theory that one species can produce an entirely different one:

"And God said, 'Let the land produce living creatures according to their kinds: livestock, creatures that move along the ground, and wild animals, each according to its kind' "(Genesis 1:24; see also 1:11 and 1:21).

"Each according to its kind." In other words, two horses might produce a horse of a different color, but they will never produce anything but horses.

Think It Through: Skeptics scoff at the biblical idea of God speaking the universe into being. "That's absurd! No one can create something from nothing." Yet many of these same scholars are willing to believe that the universe just happened. In other words, they believe *nothing* created *something* out of *nothing!*

Work It Out: The best approach to the creation/evolution controversy is not to ignore it or run away from it. Meet the issue head on. Get with a friend and study both views of origins. You may be surprised to find that the "fact" of evolution is constantly undergoing modification and is actually facing serious challenges from within the scientific community.

These books will spark your thinking: *How to Think about Evolution* by L. Duane Thurman (IVP); *Evolution: A Theory in Crisis* by Michael Denton (Adler & Adler); *Origin Science* by Norman Geisler and Kerby Anderson (Baker); and *Evolution: The Challenge of the Fossil Record* by Duane Gish (Master Books).

Nail It Down: Read Psalm 102:25.

Pray About It:

▲ ▲ ▲ ▲ FOUR

For her science term paper, Eileen wrote an essay on "Problems with Evolution: Proofs for Creation." She read tons of material, learned a lot of good things, and came away feeling more confident in her faith.

Mrs. Dubois wasn't wild about the project, but she did say later that some of Eileen's research made her think.

Good for you, Eileen! That was definitely a gutsy move.

What are the real facts of life?

Look It Up: Fortunately for us, Jesus spoke clearly on:
- The origin of the universe: "God created the world" (Mark 13:19);
- The origin of humanity: " 'But at the beginning of creation God "made them male and female" ' " (Mark 10:6).

Now, either Jesus didn't know what He was talking about, or He was telling a deliberate lie, or He was telling the truth. Those are the only options.

Think It Through: Writer Winkie Pratney correctly observed: "We are either: (1) the product of a cosmic crap-game; or (2) engineered by Wisdom, Love, and Power beyond comprehension. . . . These options have profound implications for the way you feel about yourself and others. What, for instance, do you do when overwhelmed by the beauty and awesome, orderly arrangement of a flower? Vote scenario two and say, 'Thank You, God!' Vote scenario one and be stuck with 'Praise and honor be to Gases, Geology, and Genes.' "

Work It Out: Could the marvelous world all around you have happened by chance? Do this experiment:

Print on a sheet of paper this sentence: "Our complex universe came into existence by chance, over a long period of time." Cut the sentence into individual letters and punctuation marks. Put these in a jar and shake them. Dump the letters onto the table. Do they spell anything? Do it several times. Is the result intelligible?

Maybe the characters need to fall for a longer time before they will finally end up in the right combination. Stand on a chair and drop them to the floor. Any luck?

Nail It Down: Read Acts 14:15 on Saturday, Hebrews 11:3 on Sunday.

▲ ▲ ▲ ▲ ▲ FIVE **ORIGINS** ▲ ▲ ▲ ▲ ▲

ASTROLOGY

You're standing in line at the supermarket check-out and you spot one of those horoscope books that tells you whether you're romantically compatible with a Gemini. "What's the harm?" you say. "It's just for fun."

The harm is, it *isn't* just for fun. Astrologers claim that the relative positions of the sun, moon, and stars on the day you were born determine all kinds of things about you—your personality, your desires, your destiny. (This is not to be confused with *astronomy*, which is the scientific study of the heavenly bodies.)

But nothing could be more opposed to biblical truth. The sun and moon are part of God's creation. He clearly states His purpose for putting them in the sky: "*And God said, . . . 'Let them serve as signs to mark seasons and days and years, and let them be lights in the expanse of the sky to give light on the earth.' And it was so*" (Genesis 1:14-15). Then he made the stars: "*God set them in the sky to give light on the earth, to govern the day and the night, and to separate light from darkness*" (v. 17).

To "govern" the day and the night does not mean to control what we do during the day and the night. It means that the stars help *us* to control what we do by giving us light to see at night. Furthermore, since the stars are fixed points, mankind soon realized their value in navigation systems.

God is the author of our destiny; He has already determined the plan for our lives. Those who try to learn it by consulting a horoscope (even "for fun") are in for serious trouble: "*Let your astrologers come forward, those star-gazers who make predictions month by month. . . . Surely they are like stubble; the fire will burn them up*" (Isaiah 47:13, 14). Don't play around with astrology. The people who are in it are in it for real; they're deceived and they want to deceive you too. Rather, put all your faith in Christ, to whom God has given "*all authority in heaven and on earth*" (Matthew 28:18). In making decisions, consult the Star Maker, not the stars.

 THE SEARCH FOR SATISFACTION

CRITICAL QUESTIONS

Has anyone ever told you that God loves you?
It's true! The Bible tells of a personal Creator who loves us (John 3:16) and who desires for each of us to know Him intimately (1 Timothy 2:4).

Are you aware that you are a sinner?
Unfortunately, this is also true. We all—whether in big or small ways, in thoughts or actions—have sinned (that is, rebelled) against the holy God of the universe (Romans 3:23).

According to the Bible, the penalty for this rebellion is spiritual death—that is, being separated eternally from God's life and love (Ephesians 2:12).

Do you understand that Christ died on the cross so that you can know God and experience His love and forgiveness?
This is why the story of Christ is called the "Good News." Christ paid the penalty of sin Himself! He was our substitute, experiencing the spiritual death that we deserve so that we might have eternal life (Romans 5:8).

No one and nothing else can bring us into a right relationship with God. Christ alone is able to save us from sin and death (John 14:6).

Have you ever accepted Christ's forgiveness for your sins and His gift of eternal life?
If your answer is "no" or "I'm not sure," here are your options:

(a) Humbly admit that you need a Savior and turn to God, accepting the free gift of forgiveness and eternal life that Christ offers to anyone who will believe in Him (Ephesians 2:8-9).

(b) Proudly reject Christ's love and forgiveness, thereby ensuring that you will die in your sins (John 8:24) and spend eternity apart from God (2 Thessalonians 1:9).

Think about it. Why be in the dark about your destiny when you can be sure (1 John 5:11-13)? Simply pray, "Lord Jesus, I'm trusting You right now to forgive me and to bring me into a right relationship with God. I accept Your free gift. Thank You for dying for me."

PRAYER
Tidying Up Your Prayer Life

"Lord, teach us to pray" (Luke 11:1).

"The Multiple Misconceptions of Prayer"

"Prayer is like a shopping list you take to God."
"A long blessing at breakfast also covers lunch and dinner."
"Praying with your eyes open doesn't count."
"Prayers said at church are more powerful."
"When all else fails, at least we can pray."

Saturday night, Jeannie and Louise have been chattering for an hour when Jeannie finally has to pause for breath: ". . . and did you see who she was with? I almost died," she gasps as her second wind kicks in.

Sunday morning, Jeannie seems like a different person. She sits in her pew with her hands folded, and when the pastor says, "Let us pray," she feels uncomfortable and confused. She thinks, "I feel stupid sitting here when everyone else is praying. What am I supposed to say?"

What prayer really is

Look It Up: A lot of people can relate to Jeannie. Even long-time Christians freak out at the very thought of prayer. "I can't! I don't know how." Wrong. If you can converse with a friend, you can talk to God. Prayer is simply talking to God. We communicate with our Creator through:
- Adoration—praising God for who He is (Psalm 67:3).
- Appreciation—thanking God for the blessings He gives (Psalm 100:4).
- Confession—admitting our sin to God, claiming His forgiveness, and turning away from those wrong attitudes and actions. "I prayed to the LORD my God and confessed: 'O LORD . . . we have sinned and done wrong' " (Daniel 9:4-5).
- Intercession—asking God to act in the lives of others (Ephesians 6:18).
- Supplication—telling God about our own needs (Philippians 4:6).

Think It Through: What are your conversations with God like? Of the five types of prayer listed above, which kind do you do the most? The least?

Would you feel comfortable praying out loud in front of a group? Why or why not?

Work It Out: Go to a quiet place and talk to God. Don't worry about phrasing your words perfectly. Just be honest. Pour out your thoughts and feelings. If it helps to talk out loud, do so. If you want to kneel, fine. The important thing to remember is that prayer is simply talking with God. You can do it anytime, anywhere. The point is to do it—today.

Nail It Down: Read 1 Chronicles 16:11.

⇕ ⇕ ⇕ ⇕ ⇕ ⇕ ⇕ **ONE PRAYER** ⇕ ⇕ ⇕ ⇕ ⇕ ⇕ ⇕

Melissa (I. Q. 140) is about to hit the sack for the night. As she kneels beside her bed to pray, these thoughts cross her busy mind:

"Why do I even bother? God can't possibly run the whole world, listen to everyone else who must be praying right now, *and* hear me!"

• Tony's feeling anxious about his driving exam, and he'd like to pray about it. But he's afraid to. He imagines God's voice thundering down in a fiery cloud: "How dare you bore Me with such trivial matters! Why don't you pray about something important for once!"

How God reacts to our prayers

Look It Up: For those who think that their prayers are insignificant to God, the Bible says, "No way!" Okay, it doesn't exactly say that, but read what it does say.

• God hears and delights in our prayers: "The prayer of the upright pleases him" (Proverbs 15:8).

• God loves to answer prayers: "If you, then, though you are evil, know how to give good gifts to your children, how much more will your Father in heaven give good gifts to those who ask him!" (Matthew 7:11).

• God even helps us pray: "The Spirit helps us in our weakness. We do not know what we ought to pray for, but the Spirit himself intercedes for us with groans that words cannot express" (Romans 8:26).

Think It Through: You could think of prayer as a toll-free number to heaven. Call as often as you like. There's no charge, the number always works, and you never get a busy signal or an answering machine.

Have you ever felt like God didn't care? Do today's verses help change your mind? Remember that God is your heavenly Father. He is always concerned about the things that concern you. And because His power is unlimited, you don't have to worry about His not having enough time, or being under pressure.

Work It Out: Pray through a section of Scripture. That means you take a Bible passage and say it back to God, putting what you read into your own words. This is a great way to worship God and to get to know Him better. The Psalms are especially good for this. (For starters try 103 and 145-150).

Nail It Down: Notice how Christians' prayers are described in Revelation 5:8.

Pray About It:

TWO

↕ ↕ ↕ ↕ ↕ ↕

L et's listen in on an episode of *Pathetic Moments in the History of Prayer*. Rich, a laid-back, likable kind of guy (or so he thinks) is attempting to pray:

"So, how's the Man with the plan? How's the King-meister . . . Sorry, I've been a little scarce lately. As a matter of fact, I'm probably gonna be booked up all this month too. So, um, lemme make this quick. Bless everybody (especially me)—that is, if You can hear me. Later."

How we ought to pray

Look It Up: That's what *not* to do. Now here's how we should pray:

- In Jesus' name—More than just a magical formula we tack on to the end of our prayers, this means our prayers should be consistent with all that Christ represents (John 14:13-14).
- In faith—"If you believe, you will receive whatever you ask for in prayer" (Matthew 21:22).
- Boldly—"Let us then approach the throne of grace with confidence, so that we may receive mercy and find grace to help us in our time of need" (Hebrews 4:16).
- Continuously—Morning, noon, and night (1 Thessalonians 5:17).
- Reverently—Recognizing the holiness of God (2 Chronicles 20:18).

Think It Through: How does your own prayer life stack up? If your attitude about prayer is casual, and you feel that—since you're obligated to touch base with God—you might as well get it over with, think some more. You're depriving yourself of the great relationship that God wants to have with you.

Work It Out: Start your own prayer notebook. This is a fantastic way to develop the habit of prayer . . . plus it gives you a permanent reminder of God's faithfulness!

- Divide each page into two columns.
- Write specific prayer requests (along with the date you first start praying for each item) on the left hand side of the page.
- When God answers a particular prayer, note the details in the right-hand column.
- Pray for only a few items each day.

Nail It Down: Note also that prayer also must be according to God's will (1 John 5:14-15).

THREE PRAYER

James is not happy with the way his prayer life is going. First of all, he's been praying for about two months that his parents would change their minds about letting him buy a car. They want him to wait until he is 17, and they have even offered to pay half the cost. But James doesn't want to wait.

Also, James prayed really hard that he would pass the chemistry test he forgot to study for. As he stares at the D- on his paper, he's starting to wonder if God even hears his prayers at all.

Why some prayers aren't answered

Look It Up: The Bible lists several reasons why our prayers seem to fall on deaf ears:

• Secret sin—"If I had cherished sin in my heart, the Lord would not have listened" (Psalm 66:18).

• Selfishness—"When you ask, you do not receive, because you ask with wrong motives, that you may spend what you get on your pleasures" (James 4:3).

• A lack of mercy for others (Proverbs 21:13).

• Conflict in the home (1 Peter 3:7).

• An unforgiving spirit (Mark 11:25).

• Doubt (James 1:5-7).

Think It Through: What would happen if you took the car without asking, didn't come home by curfew, and then got in a fender bender? Would you expect to walk in and talk with your parents as though nothing had happened? If you asked for an allowance at that moment, would they be likely to meet your request?

Since our parents won't accept an arrangement like that, why do we think we can expect our holy God to agree to such guidelines?

Work It Out: Is there anything you can think of that could be hindering your communication with God? Here's a course of action to help you think:

• On a piece of paper, list any situation or thing in your life that you feel God might not be pleased with. (Sometimes writing it down makes it easier to tell.)

• Share your findings with a close friend.

• Ask him or her to pray for you.

• Together try to come up with a plan to remove the barriers that restrict your communication with God.

• Agree to meet daily for prayer during the next week.

Nail It Down: Read 1 John 3:21-22.

Pray About It:

F O U R

↕ ↕ ↕ ↕ ↕

Zack Taylor can't believe how his life has changed since he began to pray.

Last year when his family moved to another city, Zack was absolutely miserable. He had no friends, he hated his new school, and he didn't think he'd ever be happy again. In desperation he began to ask God to help him.

Several months later Zack has many new friends; he's discovered that he is a talented basketball player; he leads a youth drama team at his church. But the best thing of all is something Zack didn't even ask for—he has an amazing relationship with God.

Can prayer really change things?

Look It Up: Zack didn't have to wait until he was desperate to pray, and neither do you. These promises of Jesus ought to get you excited about prayer:

• " 'I tell you the truth, if you have faith as small as a mustard seed, you can say to this mountain, "Move from here to there" and it will move. Nothing will be impossible for you' " (Matthew 17:20-21).

• " 'I tell you that if two of you on earth agree about anything you ask for, it will be done for you by my Father in heaven. For where two or three come together in my name, there am I with them'" (Matthew 18:19-20).

Think It Through: Prayer isn't just desirable—it's essential! God has ordained prayer as the primary means by which His will is accomplished on earth. This explains the old saying, "Satan trembles when he sees the weakest Christian on his knees." It also explains why influential Christians like Martin Luther, David Brainerd, and Amy Carmichael spent hours each day talking to God.

Work It Out: If you've met all the requirements from the previous four pages, you are in a position to see some amazing things. You now have the opportunity to see God move in a powerful way.

Take out your prayer notebook and ask God to do these things:
• Save a lost friend.
• Heal a shattered relationship.
• Draw a straying Christian back to Himself.
• Use you in a powerful way.
Then sit back and watch Him work!

Nail It Down: On Saturday read James 5:16-18. Read Psalm 5 on Sunday morning as a prayer to the Lord.

FIVE **PRAYER**

OBEDIENCE
Charting Your Walk with God

O bedience is an action that brings rewards. When you obey with a willing heart, you take satisfaction in a job well done. But disobedience is always a drag. Whether you disobey out of plain old rebellion, or out of laziness, you know you've let your Master down. And when you flunk out of obedience school, you may feel like packing up your bones and hitting the road. But don't be discouraged. It's never too late to learn obedience.

"The LORD your God commands you this day to follow these decrees and laws; carefully observe them with all your heart and with all your soul" (Deuteronomy 26:16).

Joel's attitude pretty much sums up the way a lot of believers feel about obedience: "I can get into most of what the Bible talks about. But when our pastor starts talking about some things, I think, no way! Nobody does that! Like, last week he started talking about 'turning the other cheek.' You tell me: If some dude punches you in the face, are you gonna just stand there and let him do it again? Not me, man! I'd knock his teeth down his throat!"

Equipment for the Christian life

Look It Up: Thanks for sharing that loving thought, Joel. Now, here's the question for you: Is obedience an option? Can believers pick and choose the commands of Christ that make sense to them . . . and just ignore the rest? Note the penetrating question Jesus asks:

" 'Why do you call me, "Lord, Lord," and do not do what I say?' " (Luke 6:46).

Do you see His point? The words *lord* and *master* were used in New Testament times to indicate an owner (Matthew 20:8), a king or ruler (Acts 25:26), or one to whom service was due (Matthew 24:45-51). To call someone *Lord* automatically meant that you were obligated to obey that person. Obedience is not an option God offers us. It's a requirement.

Think It Through: How would you respond to these commands?
- Your teacher says, "See me after school."
- A policeman motions you to pull over.
- A parent says, "Go to your room."
- A coach orders you to participate in a certain drill.

Most likely you would obey each one of these authority figures. How much more ought you to do what Jesus, the ultimate authority, tells you to do?

Work It Out: Here's a prayer to get your week off to an obedient start: "Jesus, You are Lord and I want to learn to obey You. I need to treat you as my Owner, King, and Master because that is what You are. Teach me this week the lessons I need to know. Amen."

Think of one thing Jesus commands us to do (or not to do) that you have not wholeheartedly accepted. Then begin doing that thing today!

Nail It Down: Read Matthew 7:21.

ONE **OBEDIENCE**

What's wrong with the following scene?

Jill goes to church on Sunday night and sings the hymn, "Oh How I Love Jesus." Later that night she goes home, calls a friend, and proceeds to rip to shreds someone named Leslie Adams.

"She makes me sick! I mean, what a total fake! Did you see the way she was acting around the guys? She's about as much of a Christian as my dog. I know I should just probably ignore her—and I would, if it wasn't for what she did to me last summer! But that was the worst! I'll never forgive her for that lie she told Steve about me."

Actions speak louder

Look It Up: Hey, you can't really say (or sing) about how much you love Jesus unless you're also doing what He says:

" 'If anyone loves me, he will obey my teaching. My Father will love him, and we will come to him and make our home with him' " (John 14:23).

And Jesus didn't just tell us to obey, He also gave us an example to follow:

" 'The world must learn that I love the Father and that I do exactly what my Father has commanded me' " (John 14:31).

Think It Through: Philippians 2:8 says that Christ was "obedient to death—even death on a cross!" How great is your willingness to be obedient? Are you willing to do whatever God commands—even if it means you have to suffer? If it came down to it, would you be willing to give up friends, family, a good job, a relationship, or a valued possession in order to be obedient to Christ?

Has your obedience to Christ ever cost you something you valued?

Work It Out: If you've never made a serious commitment to total obedience to Christ, here's a way to get started. Scan through the Sermon on the Mount (Matthew 5–7):

1. Pick out two or three commands of Christ that relate to weak areas in your walk with the Lord.
2. Pray, asking God to help you to be obedient in these areas.
3. Call a good Christian friend and share your commitment with him or her.
4. Ask your friend to check up on you and to keep encouraging you to do the things that Jesus commands.

Pray About It:

TWO

97

Predict the response in each situation:

Scene One: "Susan! I told you this morning to clean up your room. Why haven't you done it?"

"Sorry, Mom. I guess I just didn't feel like doing it."

Scene Two: "Tucker, get in there for Raymond."

"Coach, I'd rather not. I don't feel much like playing tonight ."

Scene Three: "Barnes, get me those sales figures!"

"Well, maybe later, Mr. Bradshaw. Right now I feel like taking a coffee break."

Feelings are irrelevant

Look It Up: Now check out these servants who were submissive to the Lord, despite all the negative emotions they must have felt.

• Noah was told to build an ark and fill it with animals. "Noah did everything just as God commanded him" (Genesis 6:22).

• Joshua was told to conquer the intimidating enemies in the land of Canaan. "As the LORD commanded his servant Moses, so Moses commanded Joshua, and Joshua did it; he left nothing undone of all that the LORD commanded Moses" (Joshua 11:15).

• Peter was told to quit preaching about Jesus . . . or else! "'We must obey God rather than men!'" (Acts 5:29).

Think It Through: Suppose you had been one of those men. Do you think you would have been confused by God's commands? Scared? Reluctant to obey?

It took Noah about 100 years to finish the ark. Do you think he felt like getting up every day and working on the project? Were there times when he was tempted to say, "God, this makes no sense! Forget it!"? Probably. Think about the implications if he'd given in to his feelings.

Work It Out: What command of God do you have difficulty obeying? The decree to remain sexually pure (1 Thessalonians 4:3)? The charge to guard your mouth (Proverbs 13:3)? The mandate to be honest (Psalm 15:2-3)?

Make a list of five positive results of obedience in each one of those areas. Get together with a Christian friend some time today and pray that you might become more obedient in every way. Then go out and obey, imitating Christ as well as the role models we discussed today—no matter how you feel!

Nail It Down: Read Luke 2:39.

THREE OBEDIENCE

You want to see some results of disobedience? Meet Gretchen, a tired 17-year-old at a surburban chemical dependency hospital:

"I literally grew up in the church. At 13 I could quote all the verses, and I knew exactly what I was supposed to do.

"But I rebelled. I thought, 'I can bend God's rules and get away with it.' Yeah, right . . . Look at me. I'm an addict who's already had two abortions. I'm telling you the truth, you pay a price when you reject what you know is right. And it's not even close to being worth it."

The dangers of disobedience

Look It Up: From cover to cover the Bible gives sobering examples of the consequences of disobedience. Read about:
- the tragedy of Adam and Eve (Genesis 3).
- the sad story of King Saul (1 Samuel 13–15).
- the downfall of King Solomon (1 Kings 11).
- the judgment of Ananias and Sapphira (Acts 5:1-10).

Then spend some time reflecting on this warning: "Do not be deceived: God cannot be mocked. A man reaps what he sows" (Galatians 6:7).

Think It Through: Can you think of times in your life when disobedience has been devastating to you? Can you ever get away with sin? If you don't see any immediate consequences after a wrong act, does that mean that there won't be any? Why or why not?

Perhaps you know someone like Gretchen. Think about how it would feel to be in her place. How can you guard yourself from getting into a situation like hers?

Work It Out: List on a sheet of paper the various problems involved with each of these acts of disobedience:
- not reading the Word
- not telling others about Christ
- gossiping and lying;
- sexual immorality; drunkenness
- refusing to pray
- failing to forgive others
- complaining about everything
- becoming obsessed with worldly wealth

Now, will you make a commitment to surrender all your attitudes and actions to Jesus? Let Him conform you to His likeness.

Nail It Down: Read 1 Samuel 12:14-15.

Pray About It:

F O U R

After a night of severe partying, Bill slips a $10 bill in the offering plate at church and thinks, "Hopefully, God will overlook some of the things I did last night!"

• Nancy feels guilty because she and her boyfriend have been getting too physical. So she turns down a chance to go with friends to the beach for the weekend and volunteers instead to work with an inner-city outreach. "Maybe this will help make up for all my mistakes," she says.

Don't try to buy God

Look It Up: Can we disobey God and then make up for it by "bribing" Him with our money or time?

Note the prophet Samuel's response when King Saul disobeyed God in his dealings with the Amalekites and then tried to cover up his sin with all sorts of sacrifices:

"'Does the LORD delight in burnt offerings and sacrifices as much as in obeying the voice of the LORD? To obey is better than sacrifice, and to heed is better than the fat of rams. For rebellion is like the sin of divination, and arrogance like the evil of idolatry'" (1 Samuel 15:22-23).

Think It Through: Imagine how the Internal Revenue Service agents would respond if, when they questioned you about the $1,000 in taxes you had failed to pay, you said, "Hey, I say the Pledge of Allegiance every day. Plus I do all I can to make this a better country!"

Does the IRS care about your sacrifices for the country, or do they want you to obey the law?

Work It Out: Perhaps you have some areas of disobedience in your life where you might be thinking, "Well, I'll make up for those little things by doing something extra great for the Lord." Forget it. God wants you to obey Him, not try to buy Him off.

What's more, it's insulting to God when we try to make up for our sins in our own way. Jesus has already paid the full price of our sin. So our sacrifices and acts of service should be offered to Him out of obedience and love—not out of guilt.

Pick one or two areas in your life that really stand out and commit to obedience . . . no matter what.

Nail It Down: On Saturday read and think about Jeremiah 7:21-28. On Sunday reflect on James 1:25.

FIVE **OBEDIENCE**

MIRACLES

Did Jesus really turn water into wine? Did the Red Sea really divide? For centuries skeptics have claimed that miracles are the superstitious beliefs of prescientific people or the psychological aberrations of mentally unstable people. But basically there are two reasons why some individuals reject miracles: intellectual arguments and moral excuses.

Intellectual Arguments. Like the 18th-century philosopher David Hume, some people base their argument on the belief that the universe functions according to predictable, unchanging natural laws. Since miracles are by definition an alteration of the laws of nature, and since nature's laws cannot be altered, miracles are therefore impossible.

Faulty Reasoning. But Hume made a big mistake. Natural law is completely uniform *only* if miracles never occur. We who believe in miracles believe nature is uniform—most of the time. But when God, the author of natural law, operates His universe differently, He can. That's what a miracle is. Miracles are merely God's exceptions to life's general rules.

Moral Excuses. God does perform miracles: He created the universe; He parted the waters of the Red Sea; He raised His Son from the dead. He gives believers new spiritual life. When skeptics say miracles are impossible—regardless of the evidence—they prove that many people will go to great intellectual lengths to suppress the truth they know in their hearts: that God created them and will one day hold them accountable for their actions. In truth, their response is nothing more than an excuse, a moral smoke screen, erected by people who want to be free of their obligation to obey God.

12 COUPLES OF THE BIBLE

E ach pair of biblical sweeties in the left column fits one of the descriptions on the right. Can you match them up?

1. David and Bathsheba

2. Moses and Zipporah

3. Esther and Xerxes

4. Samson and Delilah

5. Jacob and Rachel

6. Abraham and Sarah

7. Priscilla and Aquila

8. Mary and Joseph

9. Adam and Eve

10. Solomon and Shulamite

11. Hosea and Gomer

12. Jesus and the Church

A. They were old enough to be their son's great-grandparents.

B. Her husband was so pleased with her that he offered her half of his kingdom.

C. The Original Sinners.

D. A couple of tent-makers by trade, they worked with Paul.

E. He was a bridegroom of blood to her.

F. He bought her at the bargain-basement price of 15 shekels and some barley.

G. Blessed are those who are invited to the marriage supper of this Bridegroom and His Bride.

H. One of their children turned out perfect.

I. He learned that you should never let your girlfriend give you a haircut.

J. It was love at first sight when he spotted this bathing beauty.

K. She was her beloved's, and he was hers.

L. They were engaged for 7 years and had 2 children.

Answers: 1-J, 2-E, 3-B, 4-I, 5-L, 6-A, 7-D, 8-H, 9-C, 10-K, 11-F, 12-G.

WORSHIP
Heartbeat of the Christian

Does worship count as one of your more familiar and enjoyable experiences? If not, you might think of worship as merely:

- A sea of raised hands in a packed church building.
- Frowning faces singing somber hymns from the 17th century.
- Organ music bouncing off the walls of a huge, empty cathedral.
- People dancing and/or rolling in the aisles.

Flip the page for a fresh look at a very important topic.

"Declare the praises of him who called you out of darkness into his wonderful light" (1 Peter 2:9).

Karen is gushing over with praise for the newest Olympic figure-skating champion: "There's never been a skater like her—she's perfect. I'd give anything to take just one lesson from her!"

Chuck is gushing with praise for Karen: "She's a total babe. And she's crazy about me—she'd do anything for me. I'm serious—I think about her constantly."

Hey, Chuck and Karen, want to go to a praise meeting at church?

"Praise meeting?!" Chuck groans. "Why would we want to do that?"

Giving God the glory He deserves

Look It Up: We give out praise all the time, but no one is more worthy of our praise than God. Like the heavenly creatures that John saw in his Revelation, we should praise God as:

• Our Creator—" 'You are worthy, our Lord and God, to receive glory and honor and power, for you created all things, and by your will they were created and have their being' " (Revelation 4:11).

• Our Redeemer—"In a loud voice they sang: 'Worthy is the Lamb, who was slain, to receive power and wealth and wisdom and strength and honor and glory and praise!' " (Revelation 5:12).

The Almighty One gives us both physical and spiritual life . . . don't you think He deserves our worship?

Think It Through: Worship is not flattering God so that we can get something out of Him (Malachi 3:14). It's not an escape from the problems of life (Psalm 73:16-17, 26). And it's not an empty ritual (Matthew 15:8-9).

"Worship," writes one author, "is the believer's response of all that he is—mind, emotions, will, and body—to all that God is and says and does."

Grade yourself (A-F) in the area of worship.

Work It Out: Worship isn't an option—it's a command! God deserves it and we need it. If you don't spend time adoring the Lord, your Christian life will be shallow and ineffective. If you do learn to worship, you'll be plugged into the ultimate power source! Plus, you'll learn a lot about joy. (Remember Topic 1?)

Ask God to teach you what it means to worship this week. And invite a friend to study the subject with you.

Nail It Down: Read Revelation 5:13-14.

▪ ▪ ▪ ▪ ▪ ▪ ▪ ONE **WORSHIP** ▪ ▪ ▪ ▪

Consider these comments from a youth group discussion on worship:

Ann: "I'm more into private worship—I don't like big church meetings."

Dwayne: "I worship God. He knows I love Him. Isn't that enough? Why do I have to do anything?"

Ramona: "It gives me the creeps the way some churches get all emotional in their worship services."

Worship is a way of life!

Look It Up: Now consider what the Bible says:
• Worship is both private (Psalm 63) and public.
• Worship involves attitudes (Psalm 92:4) and actions (Hebrews 13:16).
• Worship involves the head and the heart. "God is spirit, and his worshipers must worship him in spirit and in truth" (John 4:24).

Think It Through: You can use this devotional guide in one of two ways: (a) as a quick fast-food snack; or (b) as an appetizer for a gourmet meal.

People with view (a) read hurriedly and don't bother to look up or reflect on the verses. They get only a tiny bit of spiritual nourishment and rarely have a genuine encounter with God. People with view (b) take time to linger in God's presence. They come away filled and satisfied because they have truly worshiped.

Which best describes you?

Work It Out: Take your Bible and a hymn book to a quiet place. Spend at least 30 minutes (you can do it!) worshiping God. Use these incomplete sentences to guide your thoughts:
• My two favorite psalms are _____ and _____ because _____ .
• My two favorite hymns are _____ and _____ because _____ .
• I want to praise you, God, because You are

_____
• I want to thank you, God, for these five blessings:
_____ , _____ , _____ , _____ , and _____ .

Sing softly, kneel if you like, raise your hands if you desire (1 Timothy 2:8). Quietly worship—out of love.

Nail It Down: Read Psalm 100.

Pray About It:

■ ■ ■ ■ T W O

Youth group A emphasizes good Bible studies and frequent outings. The attendance often exceeds 100. A lot of teens are keeping on track with God as a result of this youth group.

Youth group B does those same things, but it also has a special praise meeting each week. Only about 20 kids show up, but the maturity and commitment in this group seem so much deeper than in Youth group A.

The rich results of worship

Look It Up: What is it about worship that makes such a difference?

• Worship pleases God (John 4:23).

• Worship leads to service. "While they were worshiping the Lord and fasting, the Holy Spirit said, 'Set apart for me Barnabas and Saul for the work to which I have called them' " (Acts 13:2). See an additional example of this truth in Isaiah 6.

• Worship transforms us. "And we, who with unveiled faces all reflect the Lord's glory, are being transformed into his likeness with ever-increasing glory" (2 Corinthians 3:18).

What a great promise! The more we worship God, the more we will be changed from the inside out. People will be able see His light radiating from within us.

Think It Through: Does God *need* our worship? Not at all. According to Acts 17:25, He is completely self-sufficient. We worship God to give Him the glory and honor He deserves . . . and so that we might be transformed by living in His presence!

Are we suggesting that Bible studies and outings are wastes of time? By no means. What we are saying is that serious worship should be at the *heart* of every youth program. Is it in yours?

Work It Out: Ask your friends who belong to different denominations what their worship services are like. You might even plan to visit various friends' churches this month and witness their worship services.

(This project may give you some excellent opportunities to share your faith with people who, despite going to church, have not yet accepted Christ! Do it!)

Nail It Down: Read Psalm 96.

▪ ▪ ▪ ▪ ▪ ▪ THREE **WORSHIP** ▪ ▪ ▪ ▪

Will goes to a rock concert on Saturday night. And it really is a spectacular show —lasers, explosions, fire and smoke, multi-colored lights, a revolving stage, plus some amazing theatrics and stunts by the band. All Will can say (over and over again) is, "These guys are awesome! This concert is excellent!"

Sunday at noon, as the congregation streams out of church, Steve mumbles, "Man, am I ever glad that's over!" Will nods, "No kidding . . . too bad church can't be like last night."

The wonder of worship

Look It Up: Too many Christians fail to worship because they have forgotten what it means to be in awe of the mystery and the majesty of God. Catch the sense of wonder in this prayer of King David:

"When I consider your heavens, the work of your fingers, the moon and the stars, which you have set in place, what is man that you are mindful of him, the son of man that you care for him? . . . O LORD, our Lord, how majestic is your name in all the earth!" (Psalm 8:3-4, 9).

Think It Through: We say that a lot of things are awesome—a sports play, a car, a stereo system, a nice-looking member of the opposite sex. But is there anything more awesome than *God?*

Granted, few church services have the "fireworks" of a rock concert, but when was the last time you went into a worship service really expecting God to speak to you? If you were to approach worship with the same attitude of expectation you'd have for, say, a great concert, you'd come out of the service absolutely floored.

Work It Out: Some teenagers get to bed so late on Saturday night that they are too tired for church. Too drained to sing or pay attention to the sermon, they complain, "Church is so boring!" The real problem isn't church or the worship service—it's a lack of sleep.

Make the commitment this week to get to bed by 11:00 on Saturday night. Have a friend keep you accountable.

Before the service starts, tell God you really want to worship Him. Ask Him to prepare your heart, and give you a sense of wonder. You won't be disappointed.

Nail It Down: Notice the Apostle Paul's sense of wonder in Romans 11:33.

Pray About It: ⎯⎯⎯⎯⎯⎯⎯⎯⎯⎯⎯⎯⎯⎯

FOUR

W alt's high school group takes a "One Day Getaway" at the beginning of each summer. It works like this:

The students and leaders leave early in the morning for a nearby park. They spend the morning in individual worship. Some sit by the lake reading their Bibles and praying. Others walk on the mountain trails.

In the afternoon they gather for sharing and praise. Each time, Walt notes the chirping birds and the blooming flowers and says, "Hey, look! We're not the only ones worshiping God today!"

Nature worships; do you?

Look It Up: Have you ever stopped to think that nature is busy praising God? It's true:

"Praise him, sun and moon, praise him, all you shining stars. Praise him, you highest heavens and you waters above the skies. Let them praise the name of the LORD, for he commanded and they were created. He set them in place for ever and ever; he gave a decree that will never pass away. Praise the LORD from the earth, you great sea creatures and all ocean depths, lightning and hail, snow and clouds, stormy winds that do his bidding, you mountains and all hills, fruit trees and all cedars, wild animals and all cattle, small creatures and flying birds" (Psalm 148:3-10).

Think It Through: Match each part of nature to the aspect of God it reminds you of (more than one answer may apply):

____ mountains	a. God's creativity
____ clouds & rain	b. God's humor
____ thunder & lightning	c. God's wisdom
____ rivers & streams	d. God's power
____ giraffes & chimpanzees	e. God's majesty

Work It Out: Steal Walt's idea. Go by yourself or with some Christian friends to a quiet park and spend some time with God.

• Reread the verses listed in these pages on worship.
• Reflect on all the ways nature praises Him.
• Renew your commitment to be a worshiping Christian. (Begin right where you are by praising God for who He is.)

Nail It Down: On Saturday, read Psalm 19:1 and Psalm 96:11-13. In preparation for worship on Sunday, read Psalm 69:34 and Psalm 98:7-9.

■ ■ ■ ■ ■ ■ ■ FIVE **WORSHIP** ● ● ● ●

GODLINESS
The Highest Compliment of All

When some Christian teenagers were asked recently if they'd like to have the reputation of being godly, the responses were as follows:

"Godliness means you're a freak or a goody-goody."

"My friends avoid people like that."

"I think it would be great to be more like Jesus!"

"Yeah, that would be nice to have on my tombstone."

"Not now . . . maybe when I'm older."

Hmmm. Is godliness really such a bad thing? Is it something we can forget until we're older? Or is being known as a godly man or woman perhaps the highest compliment of all?

"You ought to live holy and godly lives" (2 Peter 3:11).

L ugging two huge suitcases, Dave trudges up the steps. His family has just driven 600 miles. Aunt Bonnie meets them at the door with tears in her eyes.

The living room is crammed with older people, many of them sniffling. About a million dishes of food sit on the table in the kitchen. Dave has one goal in mind—to scarf down some munchies and head for the TV set in the basement.

A white-haired woman approaches him in the kitchen. "I'm sorry about your Uncle Pete. He was a really godly man."

Looking for a good value?

Look It Up: Dave nods, grabs his food, and rushes downstairs. Under his breath, he says in a mocking voice, " 'He was a really godly man' . . . big deal! He was also sick all the time, he was little, he never finished high school, and he never had a decent job. What's so great about being godly?"

Hey, Dave, glad you asked. Check out this verse: "For physical training is of some value, but godliness has value for all things, holding promise for both the present life and the life to come" (1 Timothy 4:8).

"Value for all things" makes godliness the best value in the world (and in the next world).

Think It Through: Two jobs are available. One offers big bucks—but only until the summer ends. The other pays well now—and it promises millions in the future. Which would you be more interested in?

Godliness pays temporal *and* eternal dividends. That's not true of certain other qualities, such as physical strength, beauty, or popularity. What are some of the present blessings of a godly life? Are you enjoying these benefits? Would you describe yourself as a person who is "sold out to God"? Are you living a life that is pleasing to Him? If you are, then you can consider yourself godly.

Work It Out: List some of the things the world values. How many of these things will be valuable in the life to come?

Pray something like this: "Lord, help me to realize that godliness has value not just now but forever. Teach me what it means to be godly. Deepen my devotion for You this week. Amen."

Nail It Down: Read about godly Enoch—Genesis 5:24.

ONE **GODLINESS**

I t's late evening and Dave is still grumbling about Uncle Pete. Finally his older sister Judy can't take it anymore. She grabs his arm. "Hey, would you knock it off?! You're not making this any easier for Mom, you know!"

"Mom? What about me? I'm missing basketball camp this week and a party this weekend! I get yanked up to come to a dumb funeral —I barely even knew Uncle Pete."

"Well, I knew him. He was the neatest, most fun relative we ever had. He was a godly man."

Dave rolls his eyes.

The commotion about devotion

Look It Up: Someone said that godliness is "devotion to God which results in a life that is pleasing to Him." That's a great definition, but what exactly does devotion to God involve?

• It involves reverent worship. "'Who among the gods is like you, O LORD? Who is like you—majestic in holiness, awesome in glory, working wonders?'" (Exodus 15:11).

• It involves fervent desire. "My soul thirsts for God, for the living God. When can I go and meet with God?" (Psalm 42:2).

• It involves intimate love (Deuteronomy 6:5).

Think It Through: Do you assume that godliness means going around with a mournful, beaten-down expression, frowning on fun, wearing frumpy clothes, and trying to follow a long list of do not's?

Well, none of that is true. Godliness doesn't come from looking or acting a certain way. It's founded on a *relationship.* It comes when we fall in love with Jesus Christ—learn about Him, see how much He loves and accepts us, and realize what living for Him is all about.

Work It Out: No relationship can deepen until the participants . . .

• spend time together on a regular basis (Do you do this with God?).

• communicate openly with each other (God wants to talk to you through His Word. Do you let Him? And do you pray, telling Him what's on your mind?).

• begin to do the things that will please each other. (Are you doing things that you know He dislikes? Do you consider His desires and feelings?)

Nail It Down: Read Genesis 6:9.

Pray About It:

TWO

For about 30 minutes Judy lets Dave vent all his frustrations. Afterwards he's able to be more rational.

"I don't know what to think. I mean, I feel bad for Mom. Uncle Pete was her big brother and everything. I guess I should want to be here for her, but I'd really rather be back home with all my friends. Is that selfish?"

Judy shrugs, "I don't know what to tell you."

"I guess it sorta is . . . Hmmm, maybe if I was 'godly'—like about 50 people have told me Uncle Pete was—I wouldn't feel that way. But I guess I just don't have what it takes to be like that."

You've got what it takes!

Look It Up: Dave needs to know two important facts:
- The Bible tells us to live godly lives. "For the grace of God that brings salvation has appeared to all men. It teaches us to say 'No' to ungodliness and worldy passions, and to live self-controlled, upright and godly lives in this present age" (Titus 2:11-12).
- The Bible says that, with discipline, anyone can reach that goal: "Have nothing to do with godless myths and old wives' tales; rather, train yourself to be godly" (1 Timothy 4:7).

Think It Through: It's common to think that only a few "super-saints"—people like Billy Graham, Mother Teresa, and Uncle Pete—have what it takes to be godly. We reason, "I'll never be like them, so what's the use?"

But godliness has very little to do with how good a person you are. (In fact, many godly people do not fit the world's description of what a "good" person is at all.) The Bible says that *all* of us have sinned and fall short of God's standards; yet all of us are created with one common goal—to get to know God and to become godly people.

Godliness is a part of God's plan for your life. Would He plan something that was impossible to carry out?

Work It Out: Train yourself to be godly. Here are some practical ideas:
- Set your alarm clock 20 minutes earlier than usual to give yourself a few extra minutes with God each day.
- Use spare time during the day (driving, standing in lines, waiting in traffic, breaks at work) to pray, sing some praise songs to God, or memorize Scripture.
- Find a training buddy who will get serious with you.

Nail It Down: Notice that God has given us everything we need in order to live godly lives—2 Peter 1:3.

THREE **GODLINESS**

At the funeral for Uncle Pete, the minister starts his eulogy: "If I had to choose one word to describe Pete it would be the word *godly*."

Dave gives Judy a look like "This is too weird!"

The minister continues, "And he manifested this godliness in a number of ways. Pete was humble, always doing the unpleasant tasks that no one else wanted to do.

"And Pete was content. He didn't have much in the way of worldly possessions. Yet I never once heard him complain. As a matter of fact, he was always thanking God for the things he did have."

What godliness looks like (part 1)

Look It Up: The Bible extols the same virtues as being part of a godly lifestyle:

• Humility. "'For everyone who exalts himself will be humbled, and he who humbles himself will be exalted'" (Luke 18:14).

• Contentment. "But godliness with contentment is great gain" (1 Timothy 6:6).

• Thankfulness. "Enter his gates with thanksgiving and his courts with praise; give thanks to him and praise his name" (Psalm 100:4).

Think It Through: A father pushes his son to be a baseball player. The dad buys tons of equipment, takes the boy to batting clinics, forces him to practice fielding ground balls, and makes him go out for the team. The only problem is that the kid hates baseball. He has no desire to play.

Is he likely to enjoy it? Will he likely be a good player?

In the same way, without the foundation of a deep desire and love for God, the Christian life (and godliness) is a big drag.

Work It Out: If you feel kind of cold toward God, tell Him—He knows it and He can take it. Say, "God, if I'm honest, I just don't feel like training myself to be godly."

Then put the pressure on Him. Pray, "Even so, God, I'm asking You to do something wild in my life. Cause me to desire godliness by deepening my love for You. Amen."

Nail It Down: Read Colossians 3:12.

Pray About It:

FOUR

The minister is concluding Uncle Pete's funeral.

"I said that the best word I can think of to describe Pete Wallace is the word *godly*. Now, let me close with the best two *verses* I can think of to summarize his life. It's a familiar passage—some of you may even have it memorized. Yet it contains enough challenge for a lifetime, summing up for us what godliness is all about."

Dave looks at Judy and winks.

What godliness looks like (part 2)

Look It Up: "But the fruit of the Spirit is love, joy, peace, patience, kindness, goodness, faithfulness, gentleness and self-control" (Galatians 5:22-23).

Here's what those qualities mean:

• Love—a giving, forgiving, sacrificing spirit that acts on behalf of others.

• Joy—contagious exuberance that comes from being right with God.

• Peace—calm assurance that God is in control.

• Patience—an ability to tolerate, wait, and, if need be, suffer quietly.

• Kindness—a sincere desire to bring happiness to others.

• Goodness—doing things to bring happiness to others.

• Faithfulness—a loyal and dependable nature that others can rely on.

• Gentleness—sensitivity to respond appropriately to those who hurt.

• Self-control—an ability to manage one's desires.

Think It Through: Which of these qualities are most evident in your life? Least evident?

Work It Out: Trying to do godly things without first being devoted to God is a frustrating waste of time.

• First, go back and read the "Work It Out" section on page 113.

• Second, find a friend and agree together that for the next 18 days you will each work on building a deeper relationship with God. Spur each other on by sharing daily the things you're learning.

Nail It Down: Read 2 Timothy 3:12 on Saturday; read 1 Timothy 2:1-2 on Sunday.

. . . . FIVE **GODLINESS** . . .

VALUES

Practicing the Proper Principles

"See, I set before you today life and prosperity, death and destruction . . . . Now choose life" (Deuteronomy 30:15, 19).

Maybe the toughest decisions you face during your teenage years are the ones involving your personal values. What principles will you live by?

Childhood means everybody else tells you what to think and how to act. Adulthood means it's your call. Will you adopt the ideals of your parents? Will you launch out on your own? No one can live your life for you. You have to decide.

Here are some things to think about as you begin making the most important choices of all.

During a TV program on values, the following discussion took place:

"To me, the most important thing in the world is finding happiness. I think I'll find it in having—not a ton of stuff—but in, you know, a pretty good life. A nice car and house, a high-paying job that I enjoy, a family."

"I think each person has to choose his or her own values because what's important to you may not be important to me."

"Yeah. Values are definitely relative. My best friend thinks it's wrong to live together before marriage, and I say it's no big deal."

The vast variety of values

Look It Up: The Bible long ago predicted the numerous, different values we see in our culture:

"People will be lovers of themselves, lovers of money, boastful, proud, abusive, disobedient to their parents, ungrateful, unholy, without love, unforgiving, slanderous, without self-control, brutal, not lovers of the good, treacherous, rash, conceited, lovers of pleasure rather than lovers of God" (2 Timothy 3:2-4).

A lot of philosophies of life are represented in that passage—narcissism, hedonism, materialism, anti-authoritarianism, and racism—to name just a few.

Think It Through: Values aren't just theoretical ideals we think we're supposed to live by. They're the cherished principles that we actually practice.

If a guy says one of his values is moral purity and yet he hops in the sack every weekend with his girlfriend, is purity really that important to him?

Can you think of any values you've always said you hold, but that really aren't part of your lifestyle? Are there any values in Christianity you don't agree with, or have trouble understanding?

Work It Out: The goal today is twofold:

• First, take some time to write down your present values. Be honest and figure out what are your true convictions and conduct when it comes to:

Family? Money? Sex and dating? Friendships? God? Education? Marriage? Work? Church?

• Second, in preparing for tomorrow's reading, think about this question: "Where do values come from?"

Nail It Down: Read about the clash of values in Acts 17:16-34.

☆ ☆ ☆ ☆ ☆ ONE **VALUES** ☆ ☆ ☆ ☆ ☆

M rs. Huff asks her sociology class, "Where do we get our values?"

"I think a person's family plays a big part."

"Yeah. And your friends too."

"I say it's the media. I mean, I'm always watching TV and movies, reading magazines and books, listening to music. I'm sure all that affects me."

"Well, I get my values from my religion."

Where do we get our values?

Look It Up: Is there an ultimate source for the all the different values people have? Consider this:

The New Testament repeatedly refers to an ongoing, invisible war between God and Satan. Using established institutions, the devil is, even now, propagating false values in order to keep individuals from seeing what's really true: "The god of this age has blinded the minds of unbelievers, so that they cannot see the light of the gospel of the glory of Christ" (2 Corinthians 4:4).

Meanwhile, God is working by His Spirit, through His Word, and through His church to communicate the true values that lead to eternal life: "For God . . . made his light shine in our hearts to give us the light of the knowledge of the glory of God in the face of Christ" (2 Corinthians 4:6).

Think It Through: Are we suggesting that everyone who isn't a Christian is pro-Satan? No. Most people don't think in those terms.

What we are saying is that spiritual warfare is very real. And that the fiercest fighting is taking place in the realm of values. The enemy knows that if he can get people to reject the right principles and adopt the wrong ones, he can keep them in his camp forever!

Work It Out: Find the list of values that you made out yesterday. (If you haven't yet listed your values, take 15 minutes to do so right now.) Examine each principle closely, asking yourself two questions:

• What is the ultimate source of this value?

• Is it possible that this ideal is really a subtle trap of the Enemy to get me to focus on the wrong things?

Talk with a Christian friend about your values.

Nail It Down: Memorize Romans 12:2.

Pray About It:

☆ ☆ ☆ ☆ ☆ TWO

M rs. Huff is on her soapbox now.

"Class, here's the point: Values are a personal matter. No one else can tell you what to believe. You have to choose for yourself. It's not as important what values you adopt as it is for you to have some values and for you to be true to them.

"One other thing: Don't force your values on other people. Nothing is worse than for some narrow person to proclaim, 'My values are the right ones and anyone who disagrees is wrong.' "

Wrong or right? black or white?

Look It Up: Hmmm. That sounds like wise advice. But is it really? Not according to the Word of God. The Bible clearly labels some values good and others bad.

"See to it that no one takes you captive through hollow and deceptive philosophy, which depends on human tradition and the basic principles of this world rather than on Christ" (Colossians 2:8).

Rather than being narrow and repressive, Christianity is liberating! It guards us from being taken captive by a wrong value system.

Think It Through: Suppose a man likes to molest kids and a woman values the thrill of murder? Should they be free to live by those principles?

Without a clear idea of right and wrong, anything goes. Without a firm set of absolutes, we can't get on Hitler's case for killing six million Jews. He was simply living out his values.

If you don't accept biblical principles as absolute, what is your standard for evaluating all the contradictory philosophies of our time?

Work It Out: God does not set standards for no particular good reason. There are always solid truths behind each Scriptural principle.

List some of the more obvious "whys" for each of the following values:

• Remaining morally pure (1 Thessalonians 4:3-6).
• Having a generous attitude regarding money (1 Timothy 6:17-19).
• Obeying and respecting your parents (Colossians 3:20).
• Choosing your friends carefully (Proverbs 13:20).

Nail It Down: Read Hebrews 13:9.

★ ☆ ☆ ☆ ☆ ☆ THREE **VALUES** ☆ ☆ ☆ ☆ ☆ ☆ ★

Stacey and her friends were bombarded by values at the mall today . . . without even realizing it.

In a record store, they drooled over a poster of Michael Bolton. In the theater, they screamed at a new horror flick. In a clothing store they developed a serious case of the "I wants!" In a department store Stacey felt humiliated when a cosmetician told her that her make-up was all wrong. In the food court, the girls made fun of a fat woman who was eating a mountain of french fries.

Becoming a value evaluator

Look It Up: All day, and every day, we are hit with a barrage of different values. Statements and claims are made. Ideas and philosophies are introduced.

In the face of such a vast array of values, the Bible counsels us to become critical thinkers:

"We demolish arguments and every pretension that sets itself up against the knowledge of God, and we take captive every thought to make it obedient to Christ" (2 Corinthians 10:5).

The goal? To analyze all the ideas that come our way —keeping those that are true and good and discarding those that are shallow and stupid.

Think It Through: Do you actively guard your mind from bogus values and capture wrong thoughts as 2 Corinthians 10:5 suggests? Or is your mind a place where any and all values are entertained?

Remember the spiritual war we discussed earlier this week? Guess how the enemy makes the most headway? By attacking the fortress of your mind with a million false values!

Work It Out: Don't leave your mind unattended! Even a few minutes in neutral means you're a sitting duck for wrong thoughts.

Develop the habit of thinking critically. Begin questioning the things you see and hear. During and after movies, songs, class lectures, sermons, TV programs, textbook chapters, or conversations, ask yourself:
- What about this is true?
- What about this conflicts with my values?
- How might this undermine my values?
- How can I use this to strengthen my values?

Nail It Down: Read Acts 17:11.

Pray About It:

☆ ☆ ☆ ☆ ☆ FOUR

"Look," Pam says, "I have to have my own values. I'll never be a strong person if I'm always borrowing someone else's beliefs. I have to really feel something in my heart or it won't last.

"Besides, it makes me so mad when my parents tell me how to live, and then they don't even live like that. Like my dad goes crazy if I tell a lie, but sometimes when people call, I hear him say to my mom, 'Tell him I'm not home'!"

Values to last a lifetime

Look It Up: Wise words, Pam! You're right on target about having your own personal values. *Personal* doesn't mean "different than everyone else." It simply means you've struggled with your values until you understand not only what you believe, but also why.

Only then will you be able "to give an answer to everyone who asks you to give the reason for the hope that you have" (1 Peter 3:15).

Only then will you be able to resist the devil, "standing firm in the faith" (1 Peter 5:9).

Think It Through: Mistakes by a doctor don't nullify the principles of medicine. Incompetence by a pilot doesn't undo the laws of aerodynamics. In the same way, don't toss out good values just because a person who advocates them is inconsistent.

Don't buy the argument that basing your values on yourself makes you a free person. Everyone is influenced by *something*—his desires, his fears, or whatever. Who would you rather be led by—yourself, or God?

Work It Out: Biblical values are best. Such standards may seem old-fashioned, but they're true and they bring ultimate satisfaction. But you have to work that out for yourself.

• **Don't** stop asking why? "Why do we believe that? Why don't we do that?" Christianity can stand the scrutiny. But you'll never feel secure until you put your beliefs to the test.

• **Do** develop a close relationship with a more mature Christian (a youth leader, a counselor) who can help you as you sort through your values.

Nail It Down: Read Proverbs 14:12 on Saturday. On Sunday read about those who spread confusing values in Isaiah 5:20.

☆ ☆ ☆ ☆ ☆ ☆ FIVE **VALUES** ☆ ☆ ☆ ☆ ☆ ☆ ☆

Until a few years ago, you probably never heard the word *incest* spoken aloud, unless it was in reference to some remote primitive culture. Recently however, reports of incestuous abuse have become disturbingly common. And Christians are not excluded.

Incest is any sexual relationship between close family members (parents, grandparents, brothers, sisters, aunts, uncles, and, in this country, cousins). It is a sexual perversion, it is illegal, and it is explicitly forbidden by God in His Word (Leviticus 18:6-18; Deuteronomy 27:20-23). In the days before Moses, it was common for a man to marry his half-sister (Genesis 20:11-12) or for two sisters to marry the same man (Genesis 29:16-30). But God pronounced such practices unlawful when He gave the commandments to the Israelites at Sinai. Deuteronomy 18 lists the kinds of sexual relationships that God forbids.

However, incest did not disappear from society (2 Samuel 12-14). And centuries later the apostle Paul was astounded at the immorality going on in the community of believers in Corinth (1 Corinthians 5:1-2).

Incest usually involves an older family member treating a younger family member in a sexual way. Often the victims of the abuse are threatened or made to feel responsible for the abuse. They may feel guilty and confused. The consequences can be emotionally devastating.

If you are being (or have ever been) sexually abused by a family member, don't keep it a secret. No matter how painful it might be to tell someone, not telling anyone is worse. Remember, the victim of incest is not to blame. Incest is a criminal act and a sin against God. Until you tell someone about your problem, neither you nor the person abusing you will find the needed help. Go to a Christian whom you trust, whether in your school or in your church. That person will know how to help you. God loves you deeply and wants to heal your hurt.

INCEST

WISE ADVICE

If anyone ever "had it all," Solomon did. More smarts than the faculty of Harvard Business School put together (1 Kings 4:29-34). A bank account that would make an oil sheik drool (1 Kings 10:14-15, 23). More beautiful women available to him than to Hammer on a world tour (1 Kings 11:1-3).

And that's only part of the picture. Solomon (who ruled Israel from 970 B.C. to 930 B.C.) was a terrific writer. He was a connoisseur of fine wines (Ecclesiastes 2:3). His dinner parties resembled scenes from *Lifestyles of the Rich and Famous* (1 Kings 10:24-25). In his spare time, he built magnificent palaces, gardens, and parks (Ecclesiastes 2:4-6).

But here's the amazing thing: Solomon never found fulfillment in his unlimited possessions, power, or pleasure. (And he sure tried—read Ecclesiastes for an eye-opening look at Solomon's frantic search for satisfaction.)

No, Solomon's attempts to find deep meaning and joy in the things of this world were futile. That's why he made this statement near the end of his life:

"Here is the conclusion of the matter: Fear God and keep his commandments, for this is the whole duty of man" (Ecclesiastes 12:13).

There you have it. Solomon—the most "with it" guy who ever lived—saying, in so many words, "Take it from a guy who's tried it all: This world, despite all its glamor and glitz, cannot fill the empty place in your soul. Only a relationship with God will satisfy your deepest longings."

What about you? Have you found the ultimate fulfillment that only Christ can bring? Open your heart to Him. Ask Him to forgive your sins and fill you with His life and love. Then spend your life getting to know Him. That's the smartest move you can ever make. And that's the way to true riches.

GOOD WORKS
The Choice of a New Generation

Kids on drugs. Runaway teens. Juvenile delinquents. Young gang members turning cities into battlegrounds. High school drop-outs. Teenagers who worship Satan. Irresponsible adolescents. Children having children.

At every turn, you're constantly told your generation is a waste. Isn't it time you got together with your friends and proved the critics wrong?

"Let your light shine before men, that they may see your good deeds and praise your Father in heaven" (Matthew 5:16).

Vicky's weekend plans? A football game and party on Friday night, sleep till noon on Saturday, hang out with a few friends on Saturday night, church on Sunday morning, a nap on Sunday afternoon, homework on Sunday night.

Are you excited, Vicky?

"Well, it's not exactly the most awesome weekend in my life, but at least there's the game and Glen's party afterwards. Last weekend, I was totally bored. There was nothing to do."

Who ya gonna listen to?

Look It Up: While our culture encourages us to live totally for ourselves and do whatever we want, God's Word challenges us to spend at least some of our time looking for opportunities to do good to others:

• "Let us not become weary in doing good, for at the proper time we will reap a harvest if we do not give up" (Galatians 6:9).

• "Live such good lives among the pagans that, though they accuse you of doing wrong, they may see your good deeds and glorify God on the day he visits us" (1 Peter 2:12).

Think It Through: What about the people you know who live totally for themselves and who rarely think about helping others or doing what is right—do you really think they're happy? Would you want to trade places with any of them? Why or why not?

Are there ever really times when there is "nothing to do"? Don't you think that if you looked hard enough, you could always find at least one good deed to do for someone? What keeps you from doing good deeds on a regular basis?

Work It Out: Ask God today for the strength to "live a good life among the pagans" in your community.

Then pick one of these good works and trust that God will use it to bring glory (and maybe a lost person!) to Himself:

• Clean the entire house while your parents are out.
• Cut and stack some wood for an elderly person.
• Visit a sick classmate.
• Give two hours of free baby-sitting to a neighbor.
• Organize a food drive for a needy family.

Nail It Down: Read Galatians 6:10.

♥ • • ♥ • ♥ • ONE **GOOD WORKS**

Bernard says he became a Christian when he was eight—and maybe he really did. But you could never tell it just by looking at his life. He's totally into himself and the big party scene at school. He figures, "Hey, I believe. I've got my 'fire insurance,' so what's the big deal?"

Kirsten is scared she might not make it into heaven, so she's always doing lots of good deeds. Deep down, she hopes that all these acts of kindness will make her acceptable to God.

Works are evidence

Look It Up: Question: What's better to have—faith or works? Answer: They're both important!

"In the same way, faith by itself, if it is not accompanied by action, is dead. But someone will say, 'You have faith; I have deeds.' Show me your faith without deeds, and I will show you my faith by what I do. You believe that there is one God. Good! Even the demons believe that—and shudder" (James 2:17-18).

Question: What is preferable —to emphasize faith but not works, or works but not faith? Answer: Neither approach is accurate. Flimsy faith is dead, and so are empty, faithless works!

Think It Through: Some people imagine God as a cosmic accountant. They assume that good deeds add to our heavenly account, and bad deeds reduce it. A positive balance when you die means you go to heaven. A negative balance means you go you-know-where.

That's totally wrong. Works prove we have a relationship with God, but they are powerless to produce a relationship with God.

Work It Out: Demonstrate your faith. Convert your beliefs into behavior today. Here are some possibilities for letting your light shine:
- Run errands for someone in a nursing home.
- Give blood.
- "Man" the phones for a community hotline.
- Join a school service club.
- Become a big brother or sister to an underprivileged child.

Nail It Down: See the true basis for salvation in Romans 3:20 and Titus 3:5.

Pray About It: _____

T W O

Bored out of their minds, Marla and Janie were looking for anything to do. Just then the local orphanage called, asking for used toys and clothing. "Uh, we really don't have any kids' stuff here. Sorry," Janie said, hanging up the phone.

When Marla heard what the call was about, she said, "Why don't we call some people from church and see what we can do?" Within two hours they had rounded up three other friends and nine sacks of toys and clothes, and were on their way to the orphanage.

The good results of good works

Look It Up: Good works produce good results.
- They enrich our lives. "Command them to do good, to be rich in good deeds, and to be generous and willing to share" (1 Timothy 6:18).
- They provide an example for other believers. "In everything set them an example by doing what is good" (Titus 2:7).
- They prompt others to action. "And let us consider how we may spur one another on toward love and good deeds" (Hebrews 10:24).
- They please God. "And do not forget to do good and to share with others, for with such sacrifices God is pleased" (Hebrews 13:16).

Think It Through: According to 1 Timothy 6:17-19, which brings more security—concentrating on building a personal fortune, or dedicating your time and money to doing good works? Are you rich in good deeds?

Does your lifestyle prompt others to do what's right or does it steer them toward questionable activity?

Work It Out: Instead of seeing what you can get today, see how many ways you can give to others.
- See if you can motivate your friends to get involved in some sort of service project.
- Take the money you're about to spend on a new cassette, a weekend date, or a new sweater, and give it, instead, to a relief organization or a missionary.
- Spend an hour raking leaves in the yard of an older person in your neighborhood.
- Share your lunch with a classmate who forgot his or hers.

Nail It Down: See how the life of Christ is described in Acts 10:38.

♥ ♥ ♥ ♥ ♥ THREE **GOOD WORKS**

Sam shows up Saturday for his first day of work at Harry's Hot Dog Haven—the newest fast food restaurant in town. There are only two problems.

Number one, Sam's face and hands are smudged with grease (thanks to a quick oil change that morning). Number two, Sam hasn't even looked at his employee's manual. He doesn't have a clue about what he's supposed to do.

Harry just shakes his head. "Sam, I can't use you looking like that. And even if you were clean, you're not prepared to work!"

Getting ready for (good) work

Look It Up: Working for God requires preparation.

• We must keep our lives pure. "If a man cleanses himself . . . he will be an instrument for noble purposes, made holy, useful to the Master and prepared to do any good work" (2 Timothy 2:21).

• We must know God's Word (that is, what our "Heavenly Employer" expects). "All Scripture is God-breathed and is useful for teaching, rebuking, correcting and training in righteousness, so that the man of God may be thoroughly equipped for every good work" (2 Timothy 3:16-17).

Think It Through: The Boy Scouts' motto is: "Be prepared." That's also a good principle for Christians.

Are you prepared . . . for good works? If a situation came along today where God wanted to use you to do a certain task, would He be able to? Or would He have to say, "Well, I'd like to use _____ , but I can't. He/she is too busy sinning"; or, "I can't use_____ , he/she doesn't even know what to do"?

Work It Out: Spend a few minutes today—and every day—preparing yourself for good works.

1. Renounce sinful habits and wrong behavior. Then accept God's forgiveness and cleansing (1 John 1:9).

2. Make the Bible a bigger part of your life. Get on a regular program of listening to good preaching and teaching. Set a goal to read through the Bible in the next year. Memorize one verse a week. Ask your pastor, Sunday school teacher, or youth leader to show you how to study the Bible on your own.

That's how to be prepared.

Nail It Down: Read Titus 3:1.

Pray About It: _____

❤ ❤ ❤ ❤ FOUR

Remember Peggy, the girl from the story on Day 3? Well, ever since she and Marla organized the clothing and toy drive for the orphanage, she's cornered almost everyone in the state of Colorado to brag about "the wonderful service project I did last weekend"—the only unselfish thing she's done in over two months!

Be careful, Peggy. It sure would be sad if you sprained your arm from all that patting yourself on the back.

Loud jerks don't do good works!

Look It Up: Two final points about good deeds:

1. Doing good should be our way of life. We should meet every need that we are capable of meeting. That's the message of the Parable of the Good Samaritan (Luke 10:29-37).

2. Doing good is not something we should boast about. Jesus gave this warning: "'Be careful not to do your "acts of righteousness" before men, to be seen by them. If you do, you will have no reward from your Father in heaven. . . . But when you give to the needy, do not let your left hand know what your right hand is doing. . . . Then your Father, who sees what is done in secret, will reward you'" (Matthew 6:1, 3-4).

Think It Through: Do you regularly share your time, energy, or resources with others? If not, why not?

How do you feel when you're around people who constantly remind others of all the great deeds they've done? When you do a good deed, do you act like Peggy?

Work It Out: Practice some secret good deeds today.
• Send an unsigned note of appreciation to a teacher.
• Give your parents the gift of silence. Without telling them, don't play your stereo for a week.
• Leave some cookies anonymously for a friend.
• While no one is looking, slip some cash into the offering plate or basket at church.
• See if you can do a particular household task for a parent without them catching you.

Good deeds are more fun when you let others discover them.

Nail It Down: On Saturday, read and think about Ephesians 2:10. On Sunday, reflect on 1 Timothy 2:9-10; 5:9-10; and Titus 3:13-14.

❤ ❤ ❤ ❤ FIVE **GOOD WORKS** ❤

GIVING

Bucks, Bank Accounts, and the Bible

Which one are you?

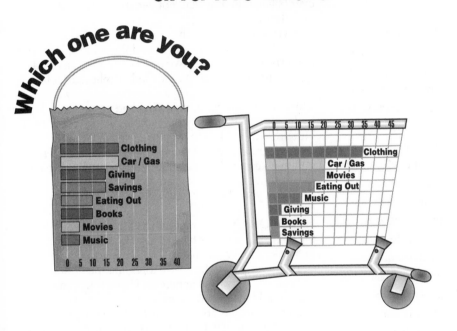

Everybody likes money, but nobody really likes being told what to do with it. Giving is a pretty sensitive subject—can't we just go on to another topic? No way! Read on to find out why giving is so important.

"The Lord Jesus himself said: 'It is more blessed to give than to receive'" (Acts 20:35).

In September, Abbey was a typical 16-year-old. Her life consisted of school, a part-time job, and involvement in youth group. Then the pretty junior was "discovered" in a mall model search. Suddenly Abbey is flying all over the country, appearing in big time fashion magazines, and making some big money!

Abbey's modeling career has changed her. She used to be known for her down-to-earth friendliness and generosity. But lately she's become awfully superior and self-centered.

Aren't you glad God isn't selfish?

Look It Up: You don't have to be a high-priced fashion model to forget two important principles:

• Christians should be thankful for God's amazing generosity. He has showered us with blessings (James 1:17)—including the ultimate gift: "For God so loved the world that he gave his one and only Son, that whoever believes in him shall not perish, but have eternal life" (John 3:16).

• We should follow the example of God's generosity. "Be imitators of God . . . and live a life of love, just as Christ loved us and gave himself up for us as a fragrant offering and sacrifice to God" (Ephesians 5:1-2).

Think It Through: Suppose God had never sent Christ to die for us. Or, imagine how different life would be if He suddenly said, "I'm tired of giving all My stuff to those ungrateful people on Earth. From now on, I'm going to keep all My blessings to Myself. No more food or sunlight or rain or answered prayers!"

Aren't you glad our God isn't as selfish as we are?

Work It Out: Spend a few minutes thanking God for the spiritual blessings He has given you. Then take time to thank Him for the material provisions you enjoy.

End your prayer time by expressing these thoughts:

"Father, You are so generous. I have much more than I could ever need. Work in my life this week so that I become like You in this area. Turn my greed into giving and my selfishness into sacrifice. In Jesus' name, Amen."

Nail It Down: Beware of getting so caught up in the gifts that you forget the Giver—Deuteronomy 8:11-18.

$ $ $ $ $ $ $ $ $ ONE GIVING $ $ $ $ $ $ $ $

Seventeen-year-old Thomas is a guy who knows what he wants, and how he plans to get it.

"I want to make money—a lot of it. I'm going to major in business, get an MBA from Harvard, then get a job with a Fortune 500 corporation."

Why is his entire plan for the future devoted to making money?

"You've got to have security, for yourself and for your family. You want to make sure their future is rock solid. You can never have too much money in the bank."

Is your security in cash or Christ?

Look It Up: You *can* put your money in the wrong bank.

"Do not store up for yourselves treasures on earth, where moth and rust destroy, and where thieves break in and steal. But store up for yourselves treasures in heaven, where moth and rust do not destroy, and where thieves do not break in and steal. For where your treasure is, there your heart will be also" (Matthew 6:19-21).

Isn't that ironic? It would seem that money provides security. Yet, the more stuff we accumulate, the more we have to worry about. Plus, these earthly "treasures" gradually steal our affections and get our minds off the things that really do matter.

Think It Through: A recent poll revealed that more than 60% of college freshmen have as their number one goal in life "to make a lot of money."

Based on the verses just cited, is that a worthy goal?

In view of the financial setbacks that are possible (being fired, being swindled, being robbed, the collapse of the stock market, runaway inflation, economic depression), is that a secure goal?

Work It Out: If you can relate to Thomas's plans, you need to make a difficult spiritual/financial transaction. You need to withdraw your security from the Bank of Wealth and deposit it all in the Bank of God. How?

• Get a concordance and look up every verse in the New Testament that has to do with money or wealth.

• Ask God to do whatever it takes to cause you to put your security in Him.

• Begin storing up treasure in heaven by giving money and time to the Lord's work.

Nail It Down: Read Matthew 6:25-34.

Pray About It:

$ $ $ $ $ $ $

TWO

Nicky and Caroline are discussing the latest lottery winner—a middle-age hairdresser from the Midwest who will be getting a check for 1.6 million dollars each of the next 25 years.

"What would it be like to have all that money?"

"I don't know, but I'd sure like to find out—hey, why don't we go right now and buy some lottery tickets?"

Wealth is there to share!

Look It Up: The desire for wealth that you don't have usually creates one of two problems:

• Frustration: "I can't get it!" "Cast but a glance at riches, and they are gone, for they will surely sprout wings and fly off to the sky like an eagle" (Proverbs 23:5).

• Ruin: "It got me!" "People who want to get rich fall into temptation and a trap and into many foolish and harmful desires that plunge men into ruin and destruction" (1 Timothy 6:9).

You can avoid both kinds of heartache. Decide now that the desire for financial success will never interfere with God's plan for your life—whatever it may be.

Think It Through: When someone once asked multi-millionaire John D. Rockefeller how much money would satisfy him, he is reported to have replied, "Just a little bit more."

That's how it usually is with those whose chief goal is to accumulate riches. They never feel like they have enough.

Work It Out: Forget the lottery. Instead, add up the approximate amount you have spent on yourself in the past month (entertainment, clothes, food, dates, etc.). Next, add up how much you have given to God (offerings and gifts, or contributions to Christian ministries). Which amount is greater?

If your spending is much greater than your giving, try to even things out. At the end of every day, dump all your change into a jar. When the container is full, roll up your coins, cash them in, and give that money to a needy family or a worthy ministry.

Nail It Down: Read about the futility of accumulating great earthly wealth—Ecclesiastes 2:20-22; Luke 12:16-21.

$ $ $ $ $ $ $ $ $ **THREE GIVING** $ $ $ $ $ $ $ $ $

Sitting with friends during the morning offering at church, Stephen pulls out a crisp $20 bill and makes a big show of dropping it into the plate.

• Benita reluctantly contributes $1 of her $10 allowance. "Great!" she thinks, "now I'll probably run out of money before Friday."

• As the plate comes her way, Clarice reasons, "I'd give my whole paycheck if I was sure God would bless me in return."

Pure gifts from pure hearts

Look It Up: People give for different reasons:
• Love for God (Luke 7:36-50). A few individuals just want to show their gratitude to God.
• Pride. These people are motivated by the desire to impress others (Matthew 6:1-4).
• Legalism. Others give, not because they want to, but because they feel they have to. "Each man should give what he has decided in his heart to give, not reluctantly or under compulsion, for God loves a cheerful giver"(2 Corinthians 9:7).
• Selfishness. These individuals use verses like Luke 6:38 ("Give, and it will be given to you") to twist the Bible's focus from giving to getting.

Think It Through: Generally speaking, those who give do prosper (Proverbs 11:25; Luke 6:38). However, we should view rewards as a *result of*, not the *reason for*, our generosity. Our motives for giving must never become self-serving (Philippians 2:3-6).
The last time you put money in the offering plate or contributed to some charitable cause, what was going through your mind? As best as you can remember, what is the true reason you gave?

Work It Out: Here are some giving ideas:
• Mail a Bible to someone in a foreign country.
• Give to a relief organization.
• Collect cans and bottles for recycling and give the money to missions.
• Guard against wrong motives in giving. How? Keep your gifts a secret. (It's also more exciting that way.)

Nail It Down: Remember—it's the attitude, not the amount. See Luke 21:1-4.

Pray About It:

FOUR

$ $ $ $ $ $ $

"Help me out here," Bridget says. "My family wants to help support this missionary in Spain, but a friend told me that we should first give 10 percent of our income to our church. Then, if we want to give over and above that amount to other people or charities, it's okay. Is that really true?"

Guidelines for giving to God

Look It Up: The New Testament says this about giving:
• Why give? " 'Freely you have received, freely give' " (Matthew 10:8).
• When, who, and how much? "On the first day of every week, each one . . . should set aside a sum of money in keeping with his income" (1 Corinthians 16:2).
• How? Willingly (2 Corinthians 8:12); generously (2 Corinthians 9:6); and cheerfully (2 Corinthians 9:7).
• To whom? Christians in need (Romans 12:13); family members (1 Timothy 5:8); widows (1 Timothy 5:16); those who minister God's Word (1 Timothy 5:17).

Think It Through: In Old Testament times, Israelites were expected to give, not one, but three tithes—one for the Levites, a second for an annual feast in Jerusalem, and a third for needy individuals. All this was in addition to various free will offerings!
The New Testament lists no explicit amount, except to say that we should give generously (2 Corinthians 9:6) and in keeping with our incomes (1 Corinthians 16:2).

Work It Out: Ten percent is a good starting point, but remember, all money ultimately belongs to God. Practice radical Christianity. In addition to your tithe:
• Take those clothes you've outgrown to an inner-city mission.
• Mail those Christian books you've already read to someone in prison.
• Give some portion of all the money you receive unexpectedly to missions.
• Devote 10% of your allowance or earnings to reaching your community for Christ.

Nail It Down: On Saturday, read Acts 4:32-35. On Sunday, reflect on Deuteronomy 16:17.

$$$$$$$$ FIVE **GIVING** $$$$$$$$

A RADICAL IDEA

It's radical! It's outrageous! It's an idea whose time has arrived.

The idea? *Wearing modest clothing at the beach.*

"Oh, no," you might be thinking. "Here we go again. This guy wants us to wear doofus-looking bathing suits."

Before you close the book, hear me out.

The age of sex: Folks, society is in big trouble. Sexually transmitted diseases are spreading like wildfire. Unfortunately, so is teen sex.

The Atlanta-based Centers for Disease Control (CDC) reported that
- nearly 40 percent of American high school students have sex regularly;
- 54 percent have had sex at least once;
- nearly 40 percent of ninth-graders and 72 percent of seniors have had intercourse.

Teens and AIDS: As of January 1993, there were 39,788 known cases of AIDS in America among adults between the ages of 20 and 29. People carry the HIV virus from eight to 10 years in their bodies before they develop symptoms of AIDS.

Think about it. If a person carries the virus for 10 years and begins experiencing symptoms at the age of 25, how old was he when he contracted the virus? It doesn't take a genius to figure it out, does it?

Bikini dipping: Our society provides plenty of stimuli for raging teen hormones. The beach, complete with oiled, scantily clothed bodies, is especially tempting.

Does this mean I'm proposing a beach ban for all Christian teens? Not at all (though given the dangers of pre-marital sex, that would be a good idea for someone who can't resist temptation at the beach).

But I am proposing this common-sense modesty guideline: If your bathing suit allows someone else to accurately discern at a glance the size and shape of all your body parts, you need to put some clothes on.

New vs. better: Don't peg me as a prude who "just doesn't understand." When I was a teenager, the so-called new morality was already firmly entrenched. I've experienced both the new morality and the common-sense biblical morality. Take it from me: The biblical morality is better — and safer.

Have fun at the beach. But be modest. Your life might depend on it. That's this editor's viewpoint. Maybe you could see it that way too.

GETTINGINTOTHE GETTINGINTOTHE TOTHE **SWING**

Ninety feet above the heads of the crowd, the trapeze swung to and fro. Two sequin-dressed, muscular figures twirled, flipped, and passed in the night. The circus band entertained the crowd as the artists performed death-defying feats in the air. Few ever hear the conversation of these artists as they work.

"Hey Larry." Swish, turn, swing back.

"Hey George." Double flip with a twist. Applause.

"Yeah?" High kick, twirl.

"Has anyone ever told you that God loves you?" Double twist, flip. Gasp!

When George turned to swing back and make the second exchange, he was met with a terrible sight. Larry's trapeze swung empty and out of control. The crowd shrieked. The band stopped.

A small crew rushed to the side of the crumpled figure. They called for a stretcher and hauled Larry away. The crowd dispersed in shock. Huggles the clown wandered about the center ring muttering and shaking his head. And overhead a stark figure loomed. George, still on his trapeze and with a tear rolling down his cheek, could be heard saying over and over, "Why did I wait? Why did I neglect Larry? If only I'd told him sooner."

What about you? Has anyone ever told you that you can actually know God—His love, forgiveness, and acceptance—and find eternal life by putting your trust in Jesus Christ?

Maybe your Christian friends are like George and have neglected to tell you the good news of Christ. If that's the case, you need to realize that His death on the cross nearly 2,000 years ago was to forgive the sins of the world. Because of Him, you can get right with God.

But it takes more than just knowing all these facts. You have to act on them. You have to quit trusting in how good you are, or what you've done, or what church you go to, and instead, depend only on Christ.

Get in the swing today. Simply pray, "God, I'm tired of pretending to be my own god. Thank You for sending Your Son, Jesus Christ, to die on the cross for my sins. Right now I am trusting Him to forgive me and give me eternal life. Please make my life whatever You want it to be."

Incidentally, Larry survived. Though he was slightly shorter and never performed again, he found a new relationship with God through Jesus Christ during his recovery. That decision made his hospital stay well worth the trouble.

WISDOM

Scrubbing Up Your Skills for Living

> of their fathers' households.
> And they lived in Gilead, in Bashan, in its towns, and in all the pasture lands of aron, as far as their borders.
> 17 All of these were enrolled in the genealogies in the days of Jotham king of Judah id in the days of Jeroboam king of Israel.
> 18 The sons of Reuben and the Gadites id the half-tribe of Manasseh, *consisting* of iliant men, men who bore shield and sword id shot with bow, and *were* skillful in battle, ere 44,760, who went to war.
> 19 And they made war against the Hagtes, Jetur, Naphish, and Nodab.
> 20 And they were helped against them. id the Hagrites and all who *were* with them ere given into their hand; for they crie'' God in the battle, and He was entreat em, because they trusted in Him.
> 21 And they took away their catt' '',000 camels, 250,000 sheep, 2,000 id 100,000 men.
> 22 For many fell slain, becaus' zs of God. And they settled in t' itil the exile.
> 23 Now the sons of the half-tr' isseh lived in the land; from Bash' ermon and Senir and Mount Hr' re numerous.
> ' And these were the heads households, even Epher, I' 'emiah, Hodaviah, and J' '-lor, famous men, hea'

> 11 and Azariah became the fath' riah, and Amariah became the father tub.
> 12 and Ahitub became the father ' dok, and Zadok became the father of Sha'
> 13 and Shallum became the father of kiah, and Hilkiah became the father of A' ah.
> 14 and Azariah became the father of S iah, and Seraiah became the father of Jeh' dak:
> 15 and Jehozadak went *along* when' LORD carried Judah and Jerusalem away' exile by Nebuchadnezzar.
> 16 The sons of Levi *were* Gershom, 'ath, and Merari.
> 17 And these are the names of the soi 'hom: Libni and Shimei.
> And the sons of Kohath *were* Amr' Hebron, and Uzziel.
> The sons of Merari *were* Mahli ' And these are the families of the ' 'ording to their fathers' *households* ' Gershom: Libni his son, Jahath ' mah his son,
> 'ah his son, Iddo his son, Zerah' 'erai his son.
> 'e sons of Kohath *were* Ammin' 'Corah his son, Assir his son, 'anah his son, Ebiasaph his s' 'n,
> 'th his son, Uriel his '

When the Bible talks about wisdom, it means more than scoring a 1400 on the SAT. Much more. Biblical wisdom involves the skills of walking right with God and understanding how to apply His truth to your life.

Do you see what that means? Someone with a 170 IQ can be a fool. A C-student can be wise.

Getting a good education is very important. Being knowledgeable will make you a more interesting person. And good grades will help you down the road.

But wisdom is the most valuable of all.

"Wisdom is supreme; therefore get wisdom. Though it cost all you have, get understanding" (Proverbs 4:7).

Bob Baxter goofed off so much during the past six weeks, he flunked chemistry. He tried talking to his teacher after school, but she said there was nothing to discuss. Really ticked off, Bob jumped in his car and spun out of the parking lot—right into a ditch!

Look at what he's facing now—an F, being dropped from the baseball team, an angry father, a huge car repair bill, higher car insurance, and the embarrassment of snickering classmates.

Bob needs some wisdom, wouldn't you say?

Wondering about wisdom

Look It Up: Some answers to your basic questions about wisdom:

Q: Where can we get ultimate wisdom?

A: From God. "For the LORD gives wisdom, and from his mouth come knowledge and understanding" (Proverbs 2:6).

Q: Who can have wisdom?

A: Anyone. "Does not wisdom call out? . . . 'To you, O men, I call out: I raise my voice to all mankind' " (Proverbs 8: 1, 4).

Q: Is wisdom easy to get?

A: No. Becoming wise involves diligent searching (Proverbs 2:1-5).

Q: Why should I pursue wisdom?

A: Because it is extremely valuable (Proverbs 3:13-18) and can save you from making huge mistakes (Proverbs 4:5-6).

Think It Through: Proverbs is probably the most practical book in the Old Testament. It contains almost 900 short sayings that are crammed with wise advice. What's the overall topic? Living for God in an ungodly world.

If you need wisdom, Proverbs is a good place to start!

Work It Out: Here's a prayer for the week:

"Lord, I need wisdom. I'm not facing exactly what Bob faces, but I do need understanding in order to deal with _____ . Work in my life this week. Change me. Show me how to live skillfully for you. Amen."

(If you want an extra challenge, make the commitment to read through the 31 chapters of Proverbs this month. A chapter a day keeps foolishness away!)

Nail It Down: Read about the purpose of Proverbs in Proverbs 1:1-6.

ONE WISDOM

On the way home from the auto body shop, Bob's mom is deathly quiet.

"I hate this!" Bob thinks. "She gives me the silent treatment and Dad is gonna scream at me for the next ten years."

But when Mrs. Baxter tells him the news, Bob's dad doesn't scream. In fact, he doesn't say anything. Bob's insides are churning. "Is he sick? Why isn't he yelling?"

After supper Mr. Baxter calmly calls from the living room, "Bob, come in here. It's time we talked."

How to spot a fool

Look It Up: Immediately Bob gets defensive. He raises his voice and starts to protest. Mr. Baxter cuts him off. "Bob, I'm not attacking you. Just listen to these verses I've been reading in Proverbs:

- "A fool finds pleasure in evil conduct" (Proverbs 10:23).
- "A fool shows his annoyance at once" (Proverbs 12:16).
- "A fool is hotheaded and reckless" (Proverbs 14:16).
- "A fool finds no pleasure in understanding but delights in airing his own opinions" (Proverbs 18:2).
- "He who trusts in himself is a fool" (Proverbs 28:26).

"Bob, according to these verses, you've been acting foolish. And you know what? Sometimes I don't act so wise myself."

Think It Through: Again and again, Proverbs points out the difference between a wise person and a fool. What about you? Looking at the list, are you being foolish in certain areas of your life?

Work It Out: Our discussion of foolishness has nothing to do with brain power. The issue is attitude. Yours could be: "No one can tell me what to do. I know best how to run my life." Or : "God, I need Your wisdom. I don't want to be a fool and do stupid things! I want to trust in You and obey You."

Get your Bible and read the listed verses again. All of them go on to show by contrast how wise people react to life's situations. After you have done that, pick one that especially describes you, and do what it says you must do to be wise.

Nail It Down: Read Proverbs 1:7.

Pray About It: ⎯⎯⎯⎯⎯⎯⎯⎯⎯⎯⎯⎯⎯

TWO

⚓⚓⚓⚓⚓⚓

As Bob tries to go to bed, he keeps rehearsing the things his dad told him earlier. He muses to himself:

"Dad's right. If I'd only listened to him and Mom, if I'd only studied harder and been more careful, none of this would have ever happened. Now, I'm off the team and I owe Mom and Dad $1000 bucks . . . "

Suddenly he sits up and clicks on the light. He reaches under his bed and pulls out a dusty Bible. "I'm stuck for now," he thinks, "but a little wisdom might keep me from getting in trouble down the line."

What to do if you want wisdom

Look It Up: Bob opens to Proverbs and reads this verse:

" 'The fear of the LORD is the beginning of wisdom, and knowledge of the Holy One is understanding'" (Proverbs 9:10).

"I wonder what 'fear of the Lord' means?" he ponders.

That phrase—and others similar to it—is found numerous times in the Bible. It doesn't refer to dread or shrinking away in horror. Instead it has to do with deep reverence and healthy respect. It means to worship in submission, obeying our good and loving God. To fear Him means that we recognize that He is the holy, all-powerful King over our lives.

The better we get to know God, the more we develop this healthy fear.

Think It Through: Ponder these related truths:

1. You'll never find true wisdom until you learn to fear God.

2. You'll never develop that reverent and respectful attitude of fear for God until you get to know Him.

3. You can't get to know God if you don't spend time with Him—in prayer and in His Word—learning what He wants.

Work It Out: Maybe, like Bob, you need some wisdom. You'll find it by learning how to fear God, which means getting to know Him. It's a lifelong process. But here's some hints to get you on the right track:

• Listen to what He says. Spend time reading and studying the Bible today. It's not just another book; it's the Word of the God of the universe!

• Do what He says. He is our King; we are His servants. Our only goal should be to obey the King.

Nail It Down: Read Job 28:28.

THREE **WISDOM**

"Hey," Bob thinks out loud, "if I work really hard the next six weeks, I could pull my chemistry grade up! And there would still be time for me to play in our last five games. Plus, if I really disciplined my time, I could get some odd jobs on the weekends and start paying back Mom and Dad!"

Bob runs back into the house to tell his parents the plan. Homer stares at him for several seconds and then wolfs down his bowl of rabbit-flavored Doggie Delight.

Use your head and plan ahead

Look It Up: Mr. and Mrs. Baxter help Bob set up a plan for achieving his goals. "I think it's great that you're planning ahead," Bob's mom notes.

She's not the only one. The Book of Proverbs encourages us all to do what Bob is doing:

• "Commit to the LORD whatever you do, and your plans will succeed" (Proverbs 16:3).

• "Make plans by seeking advice" (Proverbs 20:18).

• "The plans of the diligent lead to profit as surely as haste leads to poverty" (Proverbs 21:5).

Think It Through: Do you have some plans and goals? For this year? For the rest of your life? If you don't know where you're headed, how will you ever know when you get there?

Even though you may end up doing something completely different from what you plan, setting goals for yourself gives you a starting place. Think of your plans as a launching pad!

Work It Out: Take 30 minutes today and make out a series of plans for things you'd like to accomplish. (Make sure you consult God on this.)

You don't have to have a perfect blueprint of your entire life. And by making plans, you aren't obligated to keep them. But they'll help give you direction, and that's important. When you've finished, put the plans in a special place where you can check your progress every now and then.

Nail It Down: Make sure your plans correspond with God's—see Proverbs 19:21.

Pray About It:

FOUR

141

Five weeks down the road, Bob is well on his way to recovery. Because he's been studying an hour every night, he's now got an 81 average in chemistry! And by helping his neighbor clear some property on weekends, he's already been able pay his parents back $125 for the damage on the car.

Bob's still got a long way to go, but in just five weeks he's made some amazing strides. Because of his willingness to work hard, he's got better grades, a better feeling about himself, a better relationship with his parents, and, best of all, a closer walk with the Lord.

The wisdom in working hard

Look It Up: There is tremendous wisdom in working hard. Look at what diligence can do for you:

• "Lazy hands make a man poor, but diligent hands bring wealth" (Proverbs 10:4).

• "All hard work brings a profit, but mere talk leads only to poverty" (Proverbs 14:23).

• "He who works his land will have abundant food, but the one who chases fantasies will have his fill of poverty" (Proverbs 28:19).

The principle is clear: Wise people are hardworking individuals.

Think It Through: One high school basketball player is so good he doesn't have to put out too much effort. He excels on raw ability. Another player is equally talented, but he spends two hours each day just practicing the basics. If there's only one scholarship, guess who'll get selected? That's right . . . the hard worker.

Wisdom can be demonstrated in a lot of ways, but one big way is through working hard. How could you be more diligent in your schoolwork? In your job? In Bible study? In friendships? In prayer?

Work It Out: Start by memorizing Proverbs 14:23. As you carry that truth with you through the day, ask yourself: "Am I working hard right now, or am I just running my mouth?"

Before you go to bed tonight, review the lessons of this week and pray this prayer: "Lord, I've only started seeking wisdom in my life. Continue to show me areas where I need to grow in wisdom. Amen."

Nail It Down: On Saturday, read about the wisdom of the hard-working ant in Proverbs 30:24-25. On Sunday read 2 Thessalonians 3:6-13.

FIVE **WISDOM**

▼ ▼ ▼ ▼ SUFFERING ▼ ▼ ▼ ▼ ▼
The Point Behind the Pain

I n the short time it takes you to read this page, the ranks of the suffering will swell by several thousand.

Harsh realities (death, disaster, disease, loss, trouble, violence, hardship, misfortune, calamity, adversity, tragedy, affliction, tribulation, failure) bring harsh results (grief, heartache, depression, agony, disappointment, sorrow, sadness, pain, misery, distress, woe, anguish, despair, hurt).

Are there any answers?

"My comfort in my suffering is this: Your promise preserves my life" (Psalm 119:50).

▼ ▼

One blustery day Barbara sits sipping hot chocolate and listening to her new portable CD player. She thinks about last night: Keith told her he loves her! Things couldn't be better.

Meanwhile, the lives of other teens in the same city are filled with pain.

• Paul's parents are in the middle of a nasty divorce.

• Mike's mom has breast cancer.

• Jan's year-old nephew died last Thursday.

• Beth's father molests her.

• Tim faces major reconstructive surgery after blowing out his knee at football practice.

All over the world, all the time

Look It Up: The Bible states that as long as sinful people live in this fallen world, suffering will be a fact of life.

In the Old Testament we are told, "Yet man is born to trouble as surely as sparks fly upward" (Job 5:7).

In the New Testament, Jesus asserted, "In this world you will have trouble" (John 16:33).

Think It Through: The question really isn't "Will I suffer?" but "How will I deal with suffering?" Things are going great for Barbara right now, but circumstances can change suddenly. (How is she going to feel next week when Keith dumps her for Missy?)

Which statement describes your feelings right now?

• "Suffering is too unpleasant to even think about."

• "I'm going to pray that I never have to suffer in my whole life."

• "I know serious pain and trouble might afflict me at some point, so I want to learn how to respond in the right way."

Work It Out:

• Read today's newspaper or watch a news program on television.

• Make a list of the types of suffering that are reported: deaths, natural disasters, diseases, divorces, etc.

• Make other lists of the suffering you are aware of in your own neighborhood, church, and family.

• Then pray this: "God, the issue of suffering is an ancient puzzle. I know I won't find all the answers this week, but please at least teach me one or two new things that will help me cope, and that will also enable me to be a comfort to others who are in pain. Amen."

Nail It Down: Read 1 Thessalonians 3:2-4.

▼ ▼ ▼ ▼ ▼ ONE **SUFFERING** ▼

Maria's father, a policeman, was killed recently during a drug bust. This is how she describes her feelings:

"I know I'm supposed to believe that the Lord is in control and that He loves me. But I feel totally abandoned—like He couldn't care less. When I pray, I feel like I'm just wasting my time. It's like my prayers bounce off the ceiling. And when I try to explain it all to my friends, they just can't understand what I'm going through.

"You tell me—how is my family going to make it? What are we going to do?"

▼ ▼ ▼ ▼

The God who suffers with us

Look It Up: Notice how God responded when His chosen people were suffering as slaves in Egypt:

"I have indeed seen the misery of my people in Egypt. I have heard them crying out because of their slave drivers, and I am concerned about their suffering. So I have come down to rescue them from the hand of the Egyptians and to bring them up out of that land into a good and spacious land, a land flowing with milk and honey" (Exodus 3:7-8).

Exodus goes on to show how God used His servant Moses to deliver the people.

Think It Through: That passage tells us a lot. It tells us that when God's people are hurting: (1) He sees; (2) He hears; (3) He cares; and (4) He acts.

If you are suffering, be comforted by Exodus 3.

If you know someone who is suffering, be challenged by Exodus 3 to be a Moses in that person's life. How could God use you to help bring comfort to someone who is hurting?

Work It Out: Soothe some suffering hearts this week (and remember):

• Make personal visits. Telephone calls are okay, and notes are even better. But your physical presence means much more.

• Don't feel the need to offer profound insights or to glibly spout off a bunch of Bible verses they already know. A shoulder to cry on and a listening ear offer more comfort than a lot of talk.

• Don't make people feel guilty for feeling down. If they are sad, be sad with them (Romans 12:15).

Nail It Down: Read about the sufferings of the Son of God—Hebrews 5:7-8; 1 Peter 4:1.

Pray About It: ───────────────────

T W O

145

Maria is sobbing. Angrily she yells at Albert:

"It's not fair! How can a loving God just sit there while my father gets gunned down? If God is so good, how come my father's dead, and those drug dealers are still alive? My father was trying to make this a better place. He only cared about helping people. And now he's gone, and they're still out there pushing drugs . . . Why, Al?"

"I don't know," Al replies quietly. "I just don't have an answer."

The answer to why is who

Look It Up: In the Book of Job, Job undergoes an unbelievable series of personal tragedies (chapters 1 and 2). Friends offer all sorts of possible reasons why (chapters 3-37), but there is no comfort for Job until God finally speaks (chapters 38-41). Interestingly, God never addresses the "why?" question. He simply reveals Himself.

Reminded of God's sovereignty, Job responds, "'Surely I spoke of things I did not understand, things too wonderful for me to know. . . . My ears had heard of you but now my eyes have seen you'" (Job 42:3, 5).

It doesn't take away the pain, but somehow it helps to remember that God is good and that He's in control.

Think It Through: An artisan unveils his latest tapestry—a motley colored mass of jumbled and knotted threads. "What's that?" you mumble. The craftsman laughs and flips the ugly textile over revealing a magnificent design. You have been looking at it from the back side!

God's use of suffering in our lives is like that. From where we sit, pain is ugly and useless. But one day we'll see things from a different perspective. We'll finally understand how He weaves all our sorrow into a wonderful work of art.

Work It Out: Go to your church library or to your local Christian bookstore and get a copy of the book *Where Is God When It Hurts* by Philip Yancey. This award-winning volume gives a clear, practical explanation about why there is pain in the world and about how God uses suffering in our lives. It just may prove to be one of the most important books you'll read.

Nail It Down: Read Job 13:15-16.

▼ ▼ ▼ ▼ ▼ THREE **SUFFERING** ▼ ▼

Two tragedies, two responses:

When she was fifteen, Ellen broke her neck in an automobile accident. Paralyzed from the neck down, she has spent the last nine years in a wheelchair. Yet most of the time she is happy and joyful. She has an unusually deep walk with God. People like to be around her.

Ten years ago, Carl lost his parents in a plane crash. The initial shock and grief have turned into bitterness over the years. Carl is an alcoholic with no real friends.

A new look at an old problem

Look It Up: We see pain and suffering as horrible enemies. Yet the Bible claims that suffering has tremendous value:

• "We also rejoice in our sufferings, because we know that suffering produces perseverance; perseverance, character; and character, hope" (Romans 5:3-4).

• "I consider that our present sufferings are not worth comparing with the glory that will be revealed in us" (Romans 8:18).

Present character. Future glory. How can something that results in so much good be so bad?

Think It Through: Consider this poem by an unknown author:

> I walked a mile with pleasure;
> She chattered all the way,
> But left me none the wiser
> For all she had to say.
>
> I walked a mile with sorrow;
> And ne'er a word said she;
> But, O, the things I learned from her
> When sorrow walked with me.

Work It Out: Here are four proper reactions to pain:

Put yourself in God's hands (Psalm 31:5), remembering that He is good (Psalm 34:8).

Acknowledge that you may never fully understand the reasons for your suffering (Deuteronomy 29:29).

Include sincere thanksgiving (1 Thessalonians 5:18) and rejoicing (James 1:2) in your times of prayer.

Nourish your faith by memorizing appropriate Bible verses on suffering (e.g. 2 Corinthians 4:16-18).

Nail It Down: Read Job 23:10.

Pray About It:

FOUR

▼ ▼ ▼ ▼

Christopher could have had a dream summer—sleeping late every day and working the coveted afternoon lifeguard shift (excellent rays, lots of girl watching, and decent pay). But he surprised everyone when he said no to the pool job and yes to a missions project in Haiti.

Instead of a pleasure-filled summer of sun and fun, Christopher did back-breaking labor in the most primitive conditions . . . and he wants to go back!

Most people think Christopher is weird. But maybe he's on to something.

Choosing pain over pleasure

Look It Up: The life of Moses teaches us about tough choices:

"By faith Moses, when he had grown up, refused to be known as the son of Pharaoh's daughter. He chose to be mistreated along with the people of God rather than to enjoy the pleasures of sin for a short time. He regarded disgrace for the sake of Christ as of greater value than the treasures of Egypt, because he was looking ahead to his reward" (Hebrews 11:24-26).

Think It Through: Most people look at all their options and then take the path of least resistance. How many people do you know who are willing to choose a path of pain?

Could you make the tough choice that Christopher made? Had you been in Moses' situation, do you think you could have willingly traded a life of ease for a life of suffering? Why or why not?

Work It Out: Make a list of the decisions you'll face in the next few weeks. For instance:

• Will I trade my upcoming weekend of homecoming game celebrations for a retreat with a bunch of junior high kids because my youth pastor needs my leadership?

• Will I stand up for my Christian views on abortion and homosexuality, or will I take a hip, politically correct stance with my peers?

Chances are good that in at least some of those instances, you'll be able to choose an easy road of pleasure or a tough road of pain. Some of your options might even include suffering for being a Christian.

Nail It Down: On Saturday read Acts 5:41. On Sunday read 2 Corinthians 6:4-10.

▼ ▼ ▼ ▼ ▼ FIVE **SUFFERING** ▼ ▼

MOTIVES
A Behind-the-Scenes Look at Behavior

Did you ever feel that someone had a reason for doing something that wasn't completely clear? And you wanted to say: "What are you getting at? . . . What makes you tick? . . . What are you really after?"

Motives. What a fascinating topic. It's one thing to look at how we behave. It's another to try to understand why we act the way we do.

Let's look inside.

"Search me, O God, and know my heart; test me and know my anxious thoughts. See if there is any offensive way in me, and lead me in the way everlasting" (Psalm 139:23-24).

L et's begin our survey of motives with a comparison. Peggy, 17, is a whiz at memorizing Scripture. She even tithes on her baby-sitting money. A Christian since she was five, Peggy has never let cigarettes, alcohol, or drugs even touch her lips.

Brian, 16, accepted Christ about a year ago. No one has ever explained to him how to grow in his new faith. Though he quit smoking pot, Brian still doesn't go to church, but he would if someone invited him.

What do you suppose God thinks about Peggy? About Brian?

It's the thought that counts

Look It Up: Most people think that's a dumb question. But hold on. God says it's not just *what* we do, it's *why* we do what we do.

- "All a man's ways seem innocent to him, but motives are weighed by the LORD" (Proverbs 16:2).
- "[The Lord] will bring to light what is hidden in darkness and will expose the motives of men's hearts" (1 Corinthians 4:5).

Our reasons for doing things are just as important, if not more important, than the things themselves.

Think It Through: Remember the scribes and Pharisees of Jesus' day? They were ultra-religious. Their behavior was practically flawless. Yet Jesus criticized them more than anyone else (Matthew 6:1-18; 9:3-4). Why?

Because their motives were rotten! They liked being praised and honored. They loved being the center of attention. Basically they were selfish.

Is it possible that Brian (even though he's a new believer in Christ) might have just as pure motives as Peggy? Should we evaluate spirituality *solely* on what a person does?

Work It Out: The goal this week is to have God examine our hearts. We want to find out more about why we do the things we do. Ask God for His help:

"Father, I need You this week. I want to do the right things, but I also want to make sure that my motives are pure. Show me where I need to change so that my life can please You even more. Amen."

Nail It Down: Read more about motives and the Pharisees —Matthew 15:7-20.

▶ ▶ ▶ ▶ ▶ ▶ ONE **MOTIVES** ▶ ▶ ▶ ▶ ▶ ▶

L et's take a behind-the-scenes look at Melinda White's behavior. Like most of us, Melinda is very complex. She has numerous reasons for acting the way she does, and some of those motives are not even clear to her.

One thing about Melinda is that she uses religious activity to enhance her reputation (and to get close to cute guys). She actually believes she's fooling everyone—including God.

You can't put one over on God

Look It Up: Though we sometimes act like we can fool God, the Bible says He sees right through our facades.

• Consider the advice given to King Solomon in the Old Testament: "'Acknowledge the God of your father, and serve him with wholehearted devotion and with a willing mind, for the LORD searches every heart and understands every motive behind the thoughts'" (1 Chronicles 28:9).

• Consider this verse from the New Testament: "Jesus, knowing their evil intent, said, 'You hypocrites, why are you trying to trap me?'" (Matthew 22:18).

You might keep other people from knowing your true motives, but God knows exactly what's in your heart.

Think It Through: Are you treating God like He isn't there—like He can't see the real reasons you act the way you do?

God sees right into your heart. He's not impressed when people do the right things for the wrong reasons.

Work It Out: Get together today with your best Christian friend. Pray first, asking God for wisdom. Then try to help each other analyze why you do some of the things you do. Discuss the true motives behind your:
• dating lives
• involvement in youth group or church
• academic lives
• family interaction
• friendships

Once you have a few answers, bat this question around: "Are those really good reasons for behaving the way I do?"

Nail It Down: Read Proverbs 15:11 and Mark 2:8.

Pray About It: ——————————

TWO

151

Next we come to Danielle Long, a 15-year-old girl from the Midwest. As you can see, Danielle looks worried. A little background information: Last week her Sunday school teacher talked about motives. It was a good lesson that caused the whole class to think.

The problem now is that Danielle is afraid to do anything at all for fear that she might be acting with the wrong motives. Through extreme introspection and constant second-guessing of her every decision and action, Danielle is about to drive herself, and her friends, nuts.

Do totally pure motives exist?

Look It Up: It's good to be concerned with having pure motives. (In fact, more Christians should think about why they do what they do.) But it's not good to analyze yourself to death.

Add these twin truths to your thinking about motives:

• As sinful people, we possess impure motives. "The heart is deceitful above all things and beyond cure. Who can understand it? 'I the LORD search the heart and examine the mind'" (Jeremiah 17:9-10).

• As new creations in Christ (2 Corinthians 5:17), we can develop pure motives. "Blessed are the pure in heart, for they will see God" (Matthew 5:8).

Think It Through: Have you ever met anyone like Danielle? Are you like her?

Relax! You'll never reach perfection in this world. The point of the Christian life is growth—letting God control more and more of your attitudes and motives. As John the Baptist said, "'He must become greater; I must become less'" (John 3:30).

The more you learn to do that, the purer your heart will become.

Work It Out: Open your Bible to 1 Corinthians 13:4-8. Read the verses out loud, substituting your name every time the word *love* appears.

If the exercise makes you feel uncomfortable (because you know your motives aren't that pure), that's okay. Just pray and ask God to begin working in your heart. Ask Him to take control and cause real change in your motives.

Nail It Down: Read more about having a pure heart—Proverbs 4:20-23.

▶ ▶ ▶ ▶ ▶ ▶ THREE **MOTIVES** ▶ ▶ ▶ ▶ ▶ ▶

The 1992 Motive Watcher's Almanac might read something like this: "Researchers have thus far catalogued over 143,789 possible impure motives."

You would no doubt be impressed with such an amazing statistic. And, reading on, you might learn that:

"For the sake of simplicity, all the various motives have been categorized under five main headings: anger, jealousy, ambition (or selfishness), pride, and greed."

Can you see yourself here?

Look It Up: The statistics are right. Bad behavior almost always stems from one of five wrong reasons. Here's what the Bible says about acting out of:

• Anger—"Refrain from anger and turn from wrath" (Psalm 37:8).

• Jealousy—"A heart at peace gives life to the body, but envy rots the bones" (Proverbs 14:30).

• Ambition (or selfishness)—"Nobody should seek his own good, but the good of others" (1 Corinthians 10:24).

• Pride—"When pride comes, then comes disgrace, but with humility comes wisdom" (Proverbs 11:2).

• Greed—"The love of money is a root of all kinds of evil. Some people, eager for money, have wandered from the faith and pierced themselves with many griefs" (1 Timothy 6:10).

Think It Through: Do you react to family members out of anger or to friends out of jealousy? Is your primary concern to make yourself look better than others?

Work It Out: Think before acting. In each instance:

• Look at your options. "I can either buy this shirt or not buy it."

• Analyze the motives behind each possibility. "If I buy it, is it out of greed or to make someone jealous or to flaunt my physique? If I don't buy it, will I be proud because I have denied myself?"

• Ask God to show you the best choice to make.

• Choose the option that you feel best about.

• Keep renewing your mind daily (Romans 12:2) so God's motives will become your own!

Nail It Down: Read about impure motives in prayer—James 4:3.

Pray About It:

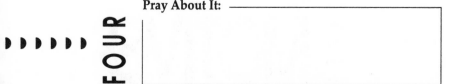

FOUR

We've learned a lot of things about motives this week, and it must be confessed, the picture so far is pretty depressing.

Wouldn't it be great if we could just zap our bad motives . . .

Picture, if you will, a gleaming contraption that looks like a helicopter cockpit with hundreds of wires coming out of it. Behind it are large, smoking containers.

This is the amazing "Motivation Modification Machine." All you have to do is step inside and all your impure motives will be changed into pure ones . . . forever!

Modifying your motives

Look It Up: Seeing your motives change is a long, difficult process. Yet there is hope. Note these verses that give us insight into the pure motives and desires of King David:

• "One thing I ask of the LORD, this is what I seek: that I may dwell in the house of the LORD all the days of my life, to gaze upon the beauty of the LORD and to seek him in his temple" (Psalm 27:4).

• "I desire to do your will, O my God; your law is within my heart" (Psalm 40:8).

Think It Through: Was David perfect? Did he always have the right motives? Obviously not. He battled (and yielded to) sinful desires just like we all do. However, during the times he diligently sought to know God and whenever he regularly meditated on God's Word, his motives were (by and large) pleasing to the Lord.

Are you spending time with God daily? Do you let His Word shape your inner thoughts and attitudes?

Work It Out: There aren't any shortcuts to having a life that is driven by right motives. Developing a pure heart is something that you will always need to work on.

Start today by getting back to basics:

• Try to memorize a couple of Bible verses each week (and spend time daily meditating on the verses).

• Hang around other Christians who desire to have pure motives.

• Pray each day for God to be glorified in your thinking and decision-making.

• Take frequent timeouts to ask yourself, "Why am I acting the way I am?"

Nail It Down: On Saturday read 1 Thessalonians 2:1-12. On Sunday read Mark 12:28-33.

▶ ▶ ▶ ▶ ▶ ▶ FIVE **MOTIVES** ▶ ▶ ▶ ▶

This Gift Can Be Yours!

REST (Matthew 11:28) • FORGIVENESS FROM SIN (Romans 6:23) • A FULL, SATISFYING, AND REWARDING LIFE NOW AND FOREVERMORE (John 10:10) • THE HOLY SPIRIT OF GOD TO COMFORT AND GUIDE YOU IN YOUR DAILY LIFE (Romans 8:9; John 14:16-17) • MEMBERSHIP IN GOD'S FAMILY AS ONE OF HIS BELOVED CHILDREN (John 1:12) • AN ETERNAL HOME IN HEAVEN (John 14:2) • A GOD-GIVEN ABILITY FOR SERVING OTHERS (1 Corinthians 12:4-11) • POWER OVER TEMPTATION AND SIN (1 Corinthians 10:13) • EARTHLY AND ETERNAL BLESSINGS (Matthew 6:33; Malachi 3:10) • PROTECTION (1 Peter 1:5) • PEACE (Isaiah 26:3; John 14:27) • STRENGTH FOR LIVING (Colossians 1:10) • THE KNOWLEDGE THAT GOD CARES FOR YOU (1 Peter 5:7) • A PERSONAL, MOMENT-BY-MOMENT RELATIONSHIP WITH THE CREATOR (John 17:3) • LIBERATION FROM GUILT (Hebrews 10:22) • SCRIPTURAL UNDERSTANDING (1 Corinthians 2:15)

ANGELS

I believe in guardian angels," Gretchen said with complete confidence. "There's no other explanation." Gretchen's certainty about the angelic world is based on a horrifying experience she had as a young mother. Returning home from shopping one day, she turned her car into a busy intersection. Suddenly, the passenger door flung open and Joel, her three-year-old son, tumbled onto the highway! Gretchen screamed, and to her horror saw that a car was barreling directly for her son!

But as fast as the incident had happened, Joel was back in the car, sitting in the seat. There wasn't a scratch on him. And there wasn't a natural explanation possible. Shaking uncontrollably, Gretchen pulled over, bowed her head, and thanked God that His angels watched over her son that day.

Do Angels Exist? God's Word is unmistakably clear: Thirty-four of the sixty-six books of the Bible contain specific references to angels. Jesus Himself affirmed the reality of these creatures (Mark 13:27, 32).

Where Do Angels Come From? Contrary to popular opinion, angels are not people who have died, gone to heaven, and "earned their wings" by performing especially good deeds. They are a special class of spirit beings created by God to serve Him (Psalm 148:2-5; Colossians 1:16). As spiritual beings, angels have spiritual bodies. And yet Scripture indicates that angels can appear in human form (Genesis 18 and 19).

Angels are busy. Angels are depicted in the Bible as God's ministers of divine work and worship. They are involved in worshiping God (Isaiah 6:3) and they serve as personal messengers from God to humans. In Old Testament times they led the Israelites out of Egypt and fought for and protected them during their wanderings.

Angels also had a major role in New Testament times. They predicted and celebrated the birth of Christ (Luke 1:26-33; 2:8-14). They ministered to Jesus after His temptation and during His passion (Matthew 4:11; Luke 22:43).They announced Christ's resurrection and ascension (Matthew 28:2-6; Acts 1:10-11). They delivered Peter from prison (Acts 5:17-20). Angelic beings also protect believers and minister to them (Hebrews 1:14).

Met Any Angels Lately? While we may wonder at these marvelous beings, we must never worship them (Colossians 2:18). And we must be friendly to strangers too . . . *"For by doing so some people have entertained angels without knowing it"* (Hebrews 13:2).

RESPONSIBILITY
The Word with a
Rotten Reputation

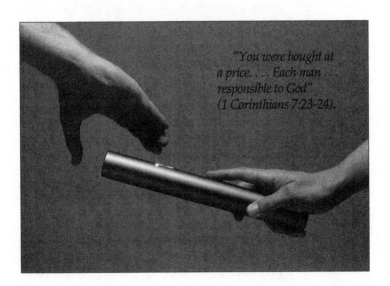

"You were bought at a price.... Each man ... responsible to God" (1 Corinthians 7:23-24).

On your list of least-favorite words, *responsibility* probably ranks right up there with Latin quiz, dental appointment, and benzoyl peroxide.

But think how life would be without any responsibilities. Your parents wouldn't have to provide you with a home; there would be no laws; you couldn't do anything that involves working together; there would be no team sports.

This week be grateful that God created us to be responsible people. Otherwise how would you reach the finish line?

Ron is on a spiritual roller coaster. Some weeks he reads his Bible and strives to do what is right. Other times he lets friends drag him into wrong situations. His problem is this:

"We have this thing at school called 'Teen Life.' It's a low-key Bible study where my non-Christian friends don't feel weird. Now my pastor wants me to get more involved in 'Teen Life.' But I won't be able to spend as much time with my friends. They'll think I don't want to hang out with them. What do you think God wants me to do?"

What advice would you give Ron?

Holy lives inside and out

Look It Up: When you cut through all the details, the bottom line issue is: "What does God want from us?" Or, "What is our responsibility to Him?" The apostle John said it like this:

"Whoever claims to live in him must walk as Jesus did" (1 John 2:6).

In other words, regardless of what else is going on in our lives, our main responsibility is to imitate Jesus. All that we say and do should reflect His love, light, and life to a world full of hate, darkness, and death.

Think It Through: Responsibility has a lot to do with love. Think about it. If God didn't love us, would He care how we lived, or how we treated one another, or whether we tried to please Him? Out of His great love, God has taken us on as His personal responsibility. His commitment to us demands that we fulfill our responsibilities to Him.

We can't really please God with our actions until our hearts are right before Him. For this reason, God is more concerned with what we *are* than what we *do*.

Work It Out: Your first responsibility to God is to love and obey Him with all your heart and all your mind. If you give yourself over to God in this way, you cannot help but become like Him, inwardly and outwardly.

You can't learn how to love or be like someone unless you spend time with that person regularly. Are you doing that? Do you make time to get to know God through His Word? Through sincere prayer?

Begin to realize your responsibility to God today. Decide to live for Him and put Him first in *all* areas of your life.

Nail It Down: Read Ephesians 1:4-6.

⚖ ⚖ ⚖ ⚖ ⚖ ⚖ ⚖ **ONE RESPONSIBILITY** ⚖

158

The East Avenue Church Youth Group is going downhill fast. Attendance is dropping. Attitudes are stale. Nobody seems interested in anything that is planned. What's Courtney's explanation?

"Everybody is too into themselves. It's like youth group is at the bottom of everyone's list of things to do. And even when people do show up —usually only for something like a party—it ends up being three or four separate little groups. We're supposed to care about each other. But obviously we don't."

To love our fellow Christians

Look It Up: Maybe Courtney's group (and yours) needs to hear about the responsibilities the Bible says we have toward fellow Christians. They are:
- To love: "Let no debt remain outstanding, except the continuing debt to love one another" (Romans 13:8).
- To set a good example: "Each of us should please his neighbor for his good, to build him up" (Romans 15:2).
- To serve (1 Peter 4:10).
- To support those in ministry (3 John 5-8).
- To help those in need (Acts 2:44-45; 4:34-35).

Think It Through: Which of your family members do you enjoy most—those who treat you badly, or those who express interest and show love to you?

Well, get this: Christians are a giant family (John 1:12)! That means we have to ask these tough questions:

In God's family, what kind of member are you? As you deal with other believers, are you fulfilling the responsibilities God has given you?

Work It Out: Pick one of these projects and do it with, or for, your siblings in God's family:
- Participate in a service project at church (a clean-up, a "Parent's Night Out" babysitting program, a ministry to church members who are bed-ridden).
- Share with a family in your church that is going through a hard time financially. Take them some homemade food, or offer to babysit or do housework.
- Support a missionary from your church.
- Take the initiative to "mend fences" between yourself and a fellow Christian with whom you've disagreed.

Nail It Down: Read 1 John 3:16-18; 4:11.

Pray About It:

TWO

Maria expresses her confusion this way:

"I don't get it. All my church ever talks about is going out and telling people about Christ—street witnessing, mission trips, weekly visitation, backyard Bible clubs, and so forth.

"But my best friend's church focuses on feeding the hungry and finding housing for street people. They mainly emphasize social issues. There the whole preaching and witnessing thing is not the main priority. My question is, which are we supposed to be doing—witnessing or helping?"

To reach out to unbelievers

Look It Up: Actually, Maria, we're supposed to be doing both. As Christians living among people who are lost and dying, we have a dual responsibility.

One priority should be to help unbelievers with their spiritual needs. As individuals who know the love and forgiveness of Jesus Christ, we have a responsibility to show others that truth (2 Corinthians 5:17-20). This was Jesus' ultimate goal: "'For the Son of Man came to seek and to save what was lost'" (Luke 19:10).

Another priority should be to help unbelievers with their physical needs. That's the lesson of the Good Samaritan: We are responsible to help people in need who cross our path.

Think It Through: Jesus came to the aid of poor, sick, and hungry individuals. And we're told to do the same. But notice that Jesus did not meet every physical need He saw (John 5:3-6).

That's because His primary purpose was to be a spiritual Savior, not a social need-meeter. As we reach out to the lost, we must not lose this perspective.

Work It Out: Are you involved in the process of bringing others to faith in Christ? You can be by:
• Praying. Make a list of unbelieving friends and relatives. Pray for their salvation.
• Giving. Support an evangelistic ministry and/or a missionary.
• Telling. Share your testimony with an unsaved friend today.
• Inviting. Be an "Andrew" and bring others to church or other Christian gatherings where they can hear about Christ (John 1:41-42).

Nail It Down: Read Romans 1:14 and Luke 10:25-37.

THREE RESPONSIBILITY

Hanging out in the park, three sophomore guys discuss their futures:

Bruce: "I'm going to Wall Street. You can make a million bucks a week just buying and trading the right stocks for a couple of hours a day."

Chad: "I'm going to win the lottery and never have to lift a finger."

Rick laughs: "You guys are full of it. You both are going to end up hustling pool and collecting welfare!"

To work hard at all we do

Look It Up: Everybody wants an easy buck. Something for nothing. Yet the Bible extols the virtue of hard work.

• "Our people must learn to devote themselves to doing what is good, in order that they may provide for daily necessities and not live unproductive lives" (Titus 3:14).

• "Even when we were with you, we gave you this rule: 'If a man will not work, he shall not eat.' We hear that some among you are idle. . . . Such people we command . . . to settle down and earn the bread they eat" (2 Thessalonians 3:10-12).

Think It Through: Some people act as though work were part of the punishment God gave Adam and Eve.

Nothing in Scripture supports this idea. God put Adam in the Garden "to work it and take care of it" *before* the Fall of mankind into sin (see Genesis 2:15). Moreover, we know that God Himself works and rests (John 5:17, Genesis 2:2-3). So there is no way we can excuse ourselves from work by reasoning that it is evil.

Work isn't evil. In fact, work is one of our God-given responsibilities.

Work It Out: You can begin fulfilling your work obligation today.

• Give your summer-time employer his money's worth. Don't goof off. Work hard right up until quitting time. And don't take his or her merchandise.

• Begin consciously rejecting the "something for nothing" philosophy that is so dominant in our culture. Refuse to take moral shortcuts (cheating in school, using steroids in athletics, shoplifting, etc.). If you want something, work hard for it.

Nail It Down: Read Ecclesiastes 5:18-19.

Pray About It:

FOUR

⚖ ⚖ ⚖ ⚖ ⚖ ⚖

Clay is getting mixed signals about how he should relate to government.

• A prominent minister recently urged Christians to pray for the death of "those liberals on the Supreme Court."

• A leader at church has been arrested for blocking the entrance to an abortion clinic.

• His dad is threatening not to pay taxes since "the government is too wasteful. Besides, some of those politicians make five or six times what I make!"

To obey the government

Look It Up: The Bible clearly outlines our responsibilities to the government:

• We are to obey our civil authorities (Romans 13:1-5).

• We are to help pay for the benefits we receive from government: "This is also why you pay taxes, for the authorities are God's servants, who give their full time to governing" (Romans 13:6).

• We are to respect our leaders. "Honor the king" (1 Peter 2:17).

• We are to pray for our political leaders (1 Timothy 2:1-2).

Think It Through: Romans 13 instructs us to live in accordance with governmental regulations. That being the case, is it ever permissible to disobey the law?

Yes—when government requires that we disobey a law of God (Acts 5:29). Read about how Queen Esther risked capital punishment to plead for the lives of her people (Esther 3–7). It is also permissible to disobey a civil law when the government fails to fulfill its lawful responsibility. (See Acts 16:35-40.)

Work It Out: You might be too young to vote, but you can fulfill your civic obligations. Here are some ways:

• Pray regularly for both national and local political leaders. Ask God to give them wisdom.

• Obey the laws that pertain to you (traffic laws, curfews, ordinances aimed specifically at minors, etc.).

• Write letters. Call your legislators. Attend political gatherings and public forums.

As a citizen and a Christian, you have an obligation to exert a godly influence in your community.

Nail It Down: On Saturday, reflect on Matthew 22:17-21; on Sunday consider the message of Titus 3:1.

⚖ ⚖ ⚖ ⚖ ⚖ ⚖ ⚖ ⚖ FIVE **RESPONSIBILITY** ⚖

✝ ✝ ✝ THE CHURCH ✝ ✝ ✝ ✝ ✝
Making Yours Even Better!

Some of the best features of the first-century church surely must have been the deep fellowship, constant prayer, powerful preaching, reverent worship, and total dependence on God. But the early church also had problems. And so do we.

Isn't it great that much of the New Testament was written to show congregations how to overcome their problems? In other words, weak churches can become stronger ones and good ones can get even better.

[Jesus replied], "I will build my church, and the gates of Hades will not overcome it" (Matthew 16:18).

✝ ✝

An older woman in Rhonda's church pulls her aside and lectures her about wearing a leather mini-skirt and loop earrings. "Young lady," the woman sternly says, "You need to dress more modestly. Haven't you read 1 Timothy 2:9-10?"

Rhonda whirls around and leaves in a huff. Later she angrily reports the episode to a friend.

"I'm sick of it! Nine million rules —don't do this, don't do that. If that's what being a Christian means, then I'll never be good enough. No matter what I do, it's always wrong."

Rules, rules, rules, and more rules!

Look It Up: By emphasizing extra-biblical rules, some believers make the same mistake that the New Testament churches in Galatia made. The result is a joyless lifestyle of bondage rather than a joyful lifestyle of liberty. Such a legalistic attitude prompted Paul to write:

- "Are you so foolish? After beginning with the Spirit, are you now trying to attain your goal by human effort?" (Galatians 3:3).
- "It is for freedom that Christ has set us free. Stand firm, then, and do not let yourselves be burdened again by a yoke of slavery" (Galatians 5:1).
- "But if you are led by the Spirit, you are not under law" (Galatians 5:18).

No wonder the book of Galatians is often called the Christian's Declaration of Independence!

Think It Through: Freedom in Christ doesn't mean we can go out and do whatever we want—God wants us to be holy. However, true holiness comes only by living in the power of the Holy Spirit, not by trying to follow an impossible list of petty rules and regulations.

In Christ, we find ourselves liberated from the mentality that says, "I have to do these 55 things to be spiritual" and free to say, "My only concern is keeping in step with the Spirit. I'm free to obey God's rules."

Work It Out: How can you avoid the trap of legalism?

1. Be an example. Model the holy, but liberated lifestyle of walking in the power of the Holy Spirit.

2. Pray that God would change the hearts of legalistic individuals in your congregation.

3. Study the book of Galatians in detail on your own.

Nail It Down: Read Galatians 5:13-26.

† † † † † † ONE **THE CHURCH** †

Jeff's church is considered the church to be seen in on Sunday morning. All the most wealthy, powerful, and well-known people in town go there.

Each week the parking lot fills up with Mercedes and Jaguars, and the pews overflow with fashionable, well-dressed men and women. Afterwards while the men talk about sports and business, the ladies discuss children and clothes.

Says Jeff: "It's just a big social event—no different from going to the country club. I don't feel like anything spiritual is even going on."

Are you infected by the world?

Look It Up: Jeff's church needs to heed the warning given to the church of Laodicea:

"I know your deeds, that you are neither cold nor hot. I wish you were either one or the other! So, because you are lukewarm—neither hot nor cold—I am about to spit you out of my mouth. You say, 'I am rich; I have acquired wealth and do not need a thing.' But you do not realize that you are wretched, pitiful, poor, blind and naked. . . . Those whom I love I rebuke and discipline. So be earnest, and repent" (Revelation 3:15-17, 19).

Think It Through: If we only go to church to be seen, to socialize, or to flaunt what we have, we've totally missed the point. The church isn't a club for the comfortable—it's a lifeboat for the drowning. Church membership isn't a credential to be listed on our resumes—it's a cause that should be a driving force in our lives.

Is your church involved *in* the world, loving the lost and helping the hurting? Or is your church *of* the world?

Work It Out: Sit down with some friends from your youth group and take the following steps:

• Discuss your lifestyles, focusing on the whole issue of worldliness. Ask the question, "Are we having an impact on the world, or is the world having an impact on us?"

• List the worldly things about your own life that need to change.

• Pray for a more spiritual focus, with less emphasis on temporal and material values.

Remember: A congregation will never change until its individual members change.

Nail It Down: Read about another worldly church in 1 Corinthians 3:1-3.

Pray About It:

✝ ✝ ✝ ✝ ✝ T W O

In only six years, Marlene's church has grown from a few families meeting in a theater, to 3,000 people with a new facility the size of a mall. Lots of people are being helped. The church's ministry just keeps on growing.

Yet Marlene is disappointed. "Sometimes I feel like a number, like I'm lost in the shuffle. I like the new worship center and my Sunday school class, but my dad hates it all. He says the church is getting to be like a big business."

Building steeples not peoples

Look It Up: Some churches, because they're doing a lot of good things, grow so big that they lose that spark that got them going in the first place. Here's what Jesus says to them:

"I know your deeds, your hard work and your perseverance. . . . You have persevered and have endured hardships for my name, and have not grown weary. Yet I hold this against you: You have forsaken your first love. Remember the height from which you have fallen! Repent and do the things you did at first. If you do not repent, I will come to you and remove your lampstand from its place" (Revelation 2:2-5).

Think It Through: Here's a truth for both individuals and churches: If you do a lot of good things for Christ but forget the main thing—loving Him and putting Him first—you're just going through the motions.

Is it more important to be concerned with programs or people? With counting the sheep or feeding them? With getting bigger or getting closer to God?

Work It Out: If your church or youth group has lost some of its friendliness, don't just sit back and criticize. Be part of the solution instead of part of the problem.

• Rekindle your own love for God. Take a whole evening or afternoon to pray and renew your commitment.

• Reach out to visitors, making it your goal to get to know one new person each week.

• Talk to your youth pastor about a small group ministry. Once-a-week get-togethers provide the chance to get to know a few other people really well. They provide intimacy even in a large congregation.

Nail It Down: Read 1 Thessalonians 3:12-13.

✝ ✝ ✝ ✝ ✝ ✝ **THREE THE CHURCH** ✝

Robert was shocked when he heard about a man and woman at his church—both regular attenders—who live together but who aren't married.

"I can't believe it!" he told one of the elders. "Hasn't anyone told them that what they're doing is wrong?"

"Robert, I don't personally approve, but who am I to judge other people? Why, we all have sin in our lives, and besides, they're very supportive members of this church."

When toleration is a bad situation

Look It Up: Loving sinners is one thing. Tolerating open sin in the church is quite another. Listen to this stern warning to the Pergamum church, a body with a "too lenient" code of conduct:

"You did not renounce your faith in me. . . . Nevertheless, I have a few things against you: You have people there who hold to the teaching of Balaam, who taught Balak to entice the Israelites to sin by eating food sacrificed to idols and by committing sexual immorality. . . . Repent therefore!" (Revelation 2:13-14, 16).

The message? God doesn't compromise when it comes to sin. Neither should His church.

Think It Through: Is it ever appropriate to leave one church and join another congregation? Yes—when you discover either one of these danger signs: A pastor who teaches things that openly contradict God's written Word, or an attitude among the body that tolerates wrong beliefs or sinful behavior.

Work It Out: As a church member, you not only have the right, but the obligation to speak out if you think such a situation might exist in your church. But first:

• ask God for wisdom in what to do;

• discuss the matter with your parents, your Sunday school teacher, or your youth minister.

As long as your motives are pure, as long as you are polite and respectful, you are perfectly justified in challenging church policies and beliefs.

As a teenager, you're not the "church of tomorrow," you're an important part of the church right now.

Nail It Down: Read Revelation 2:19-22.

Pray About It:

† † † † † † **FOUR**

Cary's dad is on the phone with the music minister. It's obvious what's up—another round between the old-time "Millerites" (loyal to the previous pastor, Dr. Miller) and the younger "Ellisites" (loyal to Rev. Ellis, the new minister).

For over a year the church has been plagued by bickering. Everything from the Sunday school schedule to the amount of money to allocate for missions has triggered a dispute.

"What difference does it make?" Cary thinks, rolling his eyes, while his dad discusses what color the new choir robes should be.

When to multiply and not divide

Look It Up: Is that what Jesus had in mind when he stated, "I will build my church" (Matthew 16:18)? Not at all. Local churches are to be marked by unity, not discord. Notice Paul's charge to the divided church at Philippi:

"Make my joy complete by being like-minded, having the same love, being one in spirit and purpose" (Philippians 2:2).

This plea came about largely because of a disagreement between two women in the congregation. Paul urged them to settle their differences:

"I plead with Euodia and I plead with Syntyche to agree with each other in the Lord" (Philippians 4:2).

Think It Through: Is there division and disharmony in your youth group? Why? What's causing the conflict? Are you a part of the problem?

You may not see how the Lord wants to use you to help resolve the situation, but it's clear that He definitely wants it resolved.

Work It Out: Don't reject God's concept of the church just because your local congregation has problems. There aren't any perfect churches.

• Pray for unity in your church.

• If you've had a disagreement with someone in the body, go to that person and resolve your differences. Jesus pronounced a special blessing on peacemakers (Matthew 5:9).

• Get the whole youth group involved. You can, under the leadership of the Holy Spirit, bring about positive changes in your church. Go for it!

Nail It Down: Read Ephesians 6:10. On Saturday read 1 Corinthians 1:10. On Sunday read 1 Peter 3:8.

† † † † † † † FIVE THE CHURCH †

♠ ♠ ♠ COMMITMENT ♠ ♠ ♠ ♠

Dedication That Makes a Difference

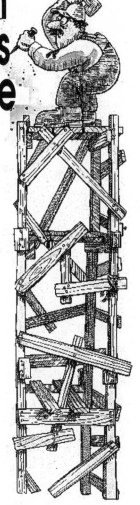

W hat if . . .
Eve had said, "Adam, you're a nice guy, but I don't think I could spend the rest of my life with you."

Moses had said, "You people find your own way to the Promised Land. I'm outta here!"

Christopher Columbus had said, "You know, maybe the world is flat. Let's turn around and go back."

What kind of world would we live in?

Commitment means no backing down, no wimping out, no giving up.

That's the kind of dedication that makes a difference.

"Commit your way to the LORD; trust in him" (Psalm 37:5).

♠ ♠

Scene 1: "You can't quit now—the youth musical is only two weeks away!"

"Look, I just decided I don't want to do it."

"But you promised . . . everybody's counting on you!"

"Well, that's too bad because I changed my mind!"

Scene 2: "Hey, see you at the beach outreach, okay?"

"Uh, Vic, something, er, came up. I can't make it."

"Can't make it!? You told me yesterday you'd be there. I'm counting on you to drive."

"I'm sorry, but something more urgent came up at the last minute."

The cult of the uncommitted

Look It Up: Commitment is a word that has lost its meaning lately. Look at how fickle people are. Job-hoppers, church-shoppers, spouse-swappers—we're always changing our minds.

This erratic pattern even invades our spiritual life. "Sure, I'm committed to Christ!" we say, as we think, "But only as long as it's convenient and comfortable." Hmm. Sounds a lot like the Jewish leaders in John 12.

"At the same time many even among the leaders believed in him [Jesus]. But because of the Pharisees they would not confess their faith for fear they would be put out of the synagogue; for they loved praise from men more than praise from God" (John 12:42-43).

Think It Through: Commitment means keeping your promises and being true to your word. In the Christian sense, it means doing the will of God—no matter what:

Check where you are in your Christian commitment.

_____ I usually only live for Christ as long as it's convenient, comfortable, and cool. (I don't want to get too radical, or be too weird!)

_____ I honestly try to do what's right regardless of my own feelings, the opinions of others, or how demanding things become.

Work It Out: Without God's direct intervention, all the vows and promises and pledges in the world won't mean a thing. To be truly committed, we need the touch of the Holy Spirit in our lives. Pray,

"Father, deepen my commitment this week. Give me a deeper love for You, a more fervent desire to know You, and a greater willingness to obey You. Amen."

Nail It Down: Read Solomon's advice to the uncommitted—Ecclesiastes 9:10.

♠ ♠ ♠ ♠ ♠ ♠ ONE COMMITMENT ♠

L ast year at this time Lisbeth was fired up for God. She was involved in youth group, talking to all her friends about Christ, and serious about renewing her mind (she had quit seeing R movies, and had begun a Bible memory plan).

Now, look at her. Oh, she's not doing anything outrageous —robbing banks, shooting drugs— but she's not doing much positive either. She makes it to youth group maybe twice a month, she rarely talks about her faith, and she doesn't even know where her Bible is!

What happened?

The danger of drifting

Look It Up: The Bible warns us not to drift from God.

"We must pay more careful attention, therefore, to what we have heard, so that we do not drift away" (Hebrews 2:1).

You need to understand that the idea of "drifting away" doesn't refer to active rebellion. It's not talking about a person who suddenly decides, "I don't want to be committed to God anymore."

No, it's talking about a gradual process. Imagine the boater who carelessly forgets to drop anchor at bedtime. By morning, he has drifted out to sea . . . and into trouble. That's what the drifting Christian is like.

Think It Through: This question may sting, but here goes: If every other Christian in the world was as committed to Christ as you are right now, how much of an impact would the church be having?

Have you floated away from God? Is your life more like: a boat purposely piloted by Christ? or a piece of driftwood aimlessly bobbing in the surf?

Work It Out: Don't let yourself get blown off course!

• First, with Colossians 3 as your map/compass, chart out your present position. (This will help you see if you are drifting.)

• Second, send out an "SOS." (This means asking God in prayer to either rescue you from your drifting, or keep you from drifting.)

• Third, look for a new crew of "sailors" (that is, a group of committed Christians) nearby who can help you keep your life in "ship-shape."

• Remember: Commitment means fighting against the tide, not going with the flow!

Nail It Down: Read Deuteronomy 4:9 and 8:11.

Pray About It:

♠ ♠ ♠ ♠ ♠   TWO

Imagine these situations:

• As he proposes marriage in the moonlight, Stewart grabs Estelle, looks deeply into her eyes and gushes, "I just want you to know that I love you with . . . sixty percent of my heart!"

• Emily turns to Reed and says, "I love you and I'm totally committed to our relationship . . . maybe. No, wait a minute. Let me think about that. Well, I sort of like you. Last Friday, I really was sure, but now I . . ."

How would you feel if someone offered you a relationship like one of these?

Do you suffer from "heart disease?"

Look It Up: The Bible often talks about the heart in describing the center of an individual's life, emotions, will, and character. A careful reading of the Word shows that true commitment takes:

• A whole heart—"Love the LORD your God with all your heart" (Deuteronomy 6:5). Committed people hold nothing back. They seek God, obey and serve Him, rejoice in Him, and thank Him with all their hearts.

• A steadfast heart—"My heart is steadfast, O God, my heart is steadfast" (Psalm 57:7). Committed people are steady, solid, and unwavering.

• A pure heart (Psalm 51:10). Committed people confess their sins quickly and move on.

Think It Through: Is your heart completely committed to the Lord? That is, are you giving Him 100 percent? If not, what areas of your life are not under His control? Why are you reluctant to give Him those things?

Does your commitment waver from day to day? What sort of situations cause you to become shaky in your walk with Christ?

Work It Out: The Great Physician specializes in healing diseased hearts. First, ask Him to search your heart (pray the prayer of Psalm 139:23-24).

Second, get on His diet and exercise program.

• Remove the dangerous "fats" (bad TV shows, nasty videos, violent movies, and raunchy magazines and music) that contribute to spiritual heart disease.

• Exercise your heart regularly—through prayer and talking about your faith.

Nail It Down: Read about King Asa's commitment to God—2 Chronicles 14-15.

♠ ♠ ♠ ♠ ♠ ♠ THREE COMMITMENT ♠

He might be lying in bed, but Jon's mind is racing.

Since trusting Christ at the end of August, Jon has been catching heat from the guys in the neighborhood. "Man, you're insane!" "You better not start getting all holy on us, Jon!"

He stares at the Bible on his bedside table. It looks so weird sitting there. He thinks of the youth meeting coming up next week (and his pledge to say a few words).

"What have I done?" he wonders.

"And what am I gonna do?"

Jon is facing one of the first tests of his commitment to Christ. What he decides now will affect his entire life.

Are you thinking of bailing out?

Look It Up: In John 6, Christ was making many of His followers uncomfortable. Their attitude was, "A little bit of this God stuff is okay, but Jesus has gone way overboard!" The result?

"From this time many of his disciples turned back and no longer followed him" (v. 66).

You can almost feel the tension and the uncertainty as Jesus turns and says to the Twelve, "'You do not want to leave too, do you?'" (v. 67). It's one of the most dramatic moments in the life of Christ.

Thankfully, Simon Peter breaks the silence (and proves his commitment) by responding boldly, "'Lord, to whom shall we go? You have the words of eternal life'" (v. 68).

Think It Through: What do you think would happen if you told God, "Here's my life. I am Yours to do with whatever You desire"?

Are you considering backing off on your Christian commitment because things are too hard, too uncertain? Before you do, consider this: Where else in the world do you expect to find real life and fulfillment? Jesus alone has the words of eternal life.

Work It Out: Read the booklet *My Heart, Christ's Home*. (Check your church library or local Christian bookstore for this IVP publication.) Afterward, get a friend to read it, and then discuss it together. Encourage each other to remain committed.

Spend a few minutes trying to envision the scene of John 6. Imagine what Jesus must have felt like. Put yourself in the place of one of the disciples.

Nail It Down: Consider the strong words of Elijah in 1 Kings 18:20-21.

Pray About It: ——————————————

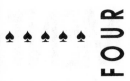

FOUR

173

Jon is talking to his Bible study leader.

"Richard, if I'm really going to be a Christian, I mean, I want to really go for it. I don't want to play games."

"That's great, Jon. So what's the problem?"

"I guess I just feel alone. I don't know too many Christians who are that serious about God. Sure would be nice to have a couple of buddies who feel the same way I do, you know? "

A classic case of commitment

Look It Up: You'd be hard-pressed to find a better role model for commitment than the apostle Paul.

He talked about commitment. "I consider everything a loss compared to the surpassing greatness of knowing Christ Jesus my Lord, for whose sake I have lost all things" (Philippians 3:8).

He demonstrated commitment. "I have . . . been in prison . . . been flogged. . . been exposed to death again and again. . . . been in danger . . . . known hunger and thirst . . . gone without food. . . . been cold and naked" (2 Corinthians 11:23-27).

Willing to give up everything. Willing to face anything. Now that's commitment!

Think It Through: Commitment is caring about and doing the will of God even if:
- People at school make fun of your faith
- It means losing a boyfriend or girlfriend
- It means a drastic change in your social life
- It means standing alone against the crowd
Could you be committed in those situations?

Work It Out: Four things will guard your commitment:
- Take time to be alone with God and His Word today and every day.
- Hang around mature believers. (Find a college student or married couple who really love God and see what makes them tick.)
- Make a public commitment to Christ and then ask your friends to hold you accountable.
- Read a chapter from *Fox's Book of Martyrs* each time your faith falters.

Nail It Down: Think more about commitment this weekend. On Saturday, read the short book of Ruth. On Sunday, consider the words of Jesus in Luke 14:25-35.

♠ ♠ ♠ ♠ ♠ ♠ FIVE **COMMITMENT** ♠